Catholicism Renewed

Power and Insight from the Charismatic Experience

Catholicism Renewed

Power and Insight from the Charismatic Experience

B. Jeffrey Anderson, PhD

With Contributions by
Leonore Misner

2021

Bible and Catechism References

Leonore M Misner

1943 – 2019

Remembering Leonore, two words come quickly to mind, *courage* and *encouragement*. Her life overflowed with both of these qualities and the Fruits of the Spirit. Decades ago, she and her husband Dale led a team of parishioners to build the beautiful stained-glass windows that bless our parish to this day. What seemed a chance meeting when they were passing through town in 2016 led to her contributions to this book. The text makes note of her witness accounts so you can see her blessing too, but the bounty of encouragement she gave me cannot be quantified.

Jeff Anderson

Acknowledgements

A long, multiyear project — and this book was one — is always a struggle, but somehow it gets done largely because the Lord sends us people who provide the help and encouragement we need. Early in the process two people stand out because they helped me find my audience and focus, Therese Boucher and Julie Sawyer. With them I must add Leonore Misner who became my co-author and always reminded me to "write with God's pen." Toward the end Fr. Joy Nellissery and Michael Janssen provided some much-needed direction, and, through it all, was the work and comments of my highly skilled and always positive editor, Claudia Volkman. In addition were the many encouraging comments and small (or not so small) favors about this or my previous books or computer fixes. In this respect I must mention Kris Ross, my sister Mary Mager (author of fine young people's books), my sons Phillip and Jacob, Bishop Robert Baker and, of course, my wife Beth who loves me, brings me coffee, and gets me through each day.

Cover art by Ellen Corbett.

Bless them Lord, and the many others not mentioned.

Also by B. Jeffrey Anderson:
The Narrow Road, A Catholic's Path to Spiritual Growth
ISBN 9 781500 480547, 2014
Intercessory Way of the Cross
ISBN 9 781544 007397, 2017

Table of Contents

Foreword:

This book is intended to help you focus on the elements of Christianity most essential for deepening your relationship with God. Much of the content is drawn from experience with the Catholic Charismatic Renewal which, unfortunately, often stands in sharp contrast to American secular culture. However, be assured it stands in good agreement with Catholic teaching, as all recent popes have affirmed. For example, Pope Francis gave the following charge to the Renewal at the Pentecost celebration of its fiftieth anniversary in 2017:

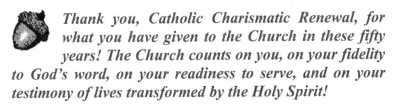 *Thank you, Catholic Charismatic Renewal, for what you have given to the Church in these fifty years! The Church counts on you, on your fidelity to God's word, on your readiness to serve, and on your testimony of lives transformed by the Holy Spirit!*

To share baptism in the Holy Spirit with everyone in the Church, to praise the Lord unceasingly, to walk together with Christians of different Churches and Ecclesial Communities in prayer and activity on behalf of those in greatest need, to serve the poor and the sick. This is what the Church and the Pope expect from you, Catholic Charismatic Renewal, but also from everyone here: all of you who have become part of this flood of grace.

PENTECOST VIGIL OF PRAYER
ADDRESS OF HIS HOLINESS
POPE FRANCIS
Circus Maximus
Saturday, 3 June 2017

Prologue: A Current of Grace

The situation today in and surrounding the American church is similar to the one Jesus faced during his earthly ministry. He often found himself speaking to a very mixed crowd—many with open hearts ready to hear and accept his message, but also many who could not (or would not) understand. His solution was to speak in parables so that those who were ready had something they could grasp, while those who were not ready would still have something to take with them, a puzzle they could work on at another time, a point of guidance the Spirit might bring to mind later at some critical juncture.[1]

Here we are, twenty centuries later, with basically the same situation: the Church needs change and renewal. Some people feel the need and are eager; others just aren't there yet. Where Jesus once used parables to carry us all along as gently and positively as possible, today he is using the charismatic gifts to get our attention and point all of us in the right direction.

In this sense the Charismatic Renewal can be seen as implementing the intent of the Second Vatican Council as expressed by Saint John XXIII in his opening address in 1962. Steering the Council away from doctrinal discussions which were sufficiently understood, he stated:

> What is needed at the present time is a new enthusiasm, a new joy and serenity of mind in the unreserved acceptance by all of the entire Christian faith, without forfeiting that accuracy and precision in its presentation. . . . What is needed, and what everyone imbued with a truly Christian, Catholic and apostolic spirit craves today, is that this

---

[1] Jesus certainly did not give up on anybody. Even in Matthew 21, he is still offering parables to the most hardhearted Pharisees, those who want to kill him.

doctrine shall be more widely known, more deeply understood, and more penetrating in its effects on men's moral lives."[2]

No one could have foreseen it at the time of the Council, but when the Holy Spirit touched the lives of a small group of college students from Duquesne University on a weekend retreat in February 1967, a current of grace was set in motion to fulfill the vision of Saint John XXIII. That event led to the advent of the Catholic Charismatic Renewal, which, just over fifty years since its inception, has touched the lives of an estimated 150 million Catholics worldwide. Once seen as a "movement," it is now regarded as a **"current of grace"** *within* **the Church[3], officially approved and encouraged by each succeeding papacy.**

 But this book is not about the renewal process per se— rather, it is about the fruits already evident from that "current of grace." This powerful grace allows us to see clearly where before it was far too easy to miss significant points about the fundamentals of Christianity and of the Church. The fundamentals have always been there but now, due to the Renewal, we can experience them more personally, more powerfully, and more deeply rooted in God's love. It is about the spiritual realities that are available to enrich all our lives now, realities that heal and strengthen and grow our faith. In short, it is about the Gospel, that *really good* news.

Growing spiritually often seems like trying to find your way home when you are lost in the woods, frustrated. . . If I could just find the path? Jesus tells us to follow the path on good soil, the one less traveled, constricted, behind a narrow gate. Frustrating? Yes, it can be. The trail markers all appear similar, all are marked "do this."

---

[2] Pope John XXIII, Opening Address to the Vatican Council II, October 11, 1962.
[3] Pope Francis, 2017 address on the occasion of the 50th anniversary of the Catholic Charismatic Renewal

The answer lies in patience, persistence, and, of course, trust in God. It is the Holy Spirit that brings you through. The process is unique to each person, so there is no cookbook to suggest an ordering of the steps.

What a blessing when the trail marks are all present, upright, clear, and in good light! That is where this book comes in. With explanations in simple language and multiple faith-building examples from both my life and that of my co-author, Leonore Misner, the path, (your perception of the Gospel), will become much clearer. The Spirit is teaching you how to recognize the true markers. The experience (witness) develops and matures your confidence (faith). It takes patience, time, and concentration (prayer). And yes, truly the walk lasts a lifetime, but it is well worth the effort.

First Steps

Some basic ideas on spiritual growth and illustrations on why the Good News is really good news.

A Key to the Door

The kingdom of heaven is like a treasure buried in a field, which a person finds and hides again, and out of joy goes and sells all that he has and buys that field. (Matthew 13:44)

How do we obtain spiritual understanding; how do we enter the realm of God? The approach is quite different from the way we normally think of things, but it is not particularly difficult. Jesus gives us a good summary in Matthew 13:44–46. He describes a man out in a field who discovers a treasure of great value. He hides it and goes rejoicing to sell all that he has and buy the field. Similarly, a pearl merchant searches and finds a pearl of extraordinary value. He also sells all he has and buys the pearl. Notice in both cases the joy and excitement; both men realize the treasure is not only of extreme value, it is deep in the heart and everlasting. They experience without any doubt that God loves them.

 There are three key steps in what Jesus is teaching us:

1. **The treasure must be noticed or, in some cases (e.g., the pearl merchant) sought after and found. The underlying principle here is that we must desire the treasure in order to obtain it.** We must want it enough to be watchful, to search for it, to ask for it. God always plays the gentleman, never coercing or pressuring us. Rather, he seeks our love freely given. He does not want to go a single step forward without our participation and willingness. When we lose interest, he stops and waits, encouraging our returned interest in every way possible.

2. **The treasure must be recognized for what it is, an invitation to be loved by the greatest, most intimate, truest lover of all, God himself, the Holy Spirit present to us.** Observe: the love comes now, in this life, and, we believe, even more completely in the next. Scripture describes it as the foretaste, the first payment of heaven

9

(see Ephesians 1:13–14; 2 Corinthians 1:21–22, 5:4–5). No wonder the purchase is made with great joy and expectancy.

3. **It must be properly purchased. The purchase involves giving up what one has, or "denying yourself," but, not with a heavy heart**. The value of the treasure overwhelms any sense of loss. In day-to-day practice, this means recognizing that God's plan for you is a lot better, and more important, than your plan. In practice this does not mean that your plan must be completely set aside; rather, it just drops in priority; God's priority comes first. Also, remember God's plan is uniquely developed for you, a perfect fit. It doesn't take long before you realize that it is clearly best, and the fruits bear that out.

There are two important and complementary aspects of the "purchase price," the denying oneself in favor of following God's plan. The first is dependence on God; the other is obedience. God is the master builder, and he knows how the plan needs to come together. As his assistants, we need to support him in that effort. When it seems that there are more problems than progress, we might recheck our discernment, but we must retain our trust in God.

Our obedience to his wishes, his way of doing things, enables him to shape and control the process to bring about the best result, whether in us or our children or in others around us. Obedience has two important benefits. First, it keeps us from wandering out into the weeds of life—acting in unloving ways that harm others or separate us from the community. Second, it trains us to be perceptive to the leadings of the Spirit—to grow in discernment and thus in effectiveness in serving God.

Here there is also a subtle but very significant truth: part of the assembly process, the work God is doing within us, is teaching us how to do the assembly. While God is doing the building within us, he is also preparing us to help build others. Suddenly the importance of obedience becomes very evident. It is not just our spiritual growth that is at stake; it is the growth of community as well. God's "yoke is easy and his burden light," but it is very important.

Your Daily Life

In practice what this all means is that our daily walk is by discernment more than choice. A simple example: when someone asks you "What do you want?" you realize that is the wrong question. The right question is "What does God have going here? What does *he* want?" We pause, consider, and listen for his answer, and proceed accordingly. If God doesn't answer, then we are free to answer the first question. Again, God's plan takes priority over ours.

In practice, we know that spiritual growth, entering the kingdom, is a lifelong process, generally with small repetitive steps as we find bits of the treasure and buy it a little at a time. The prior experiences build our faith and alleviate fear of the price. We must be patient, yet occasionally there is a big jump. Interestingly, age does not seem to be a factor. I have known very young children, grade schoolers, who show clear evidence of deep faith and a close relationship with God. On the other hand, I also remember a senior NASA manager, the only one who ever gave me (gently) a hard time about being Catholic. Several years after he retired, I was surprised while climbing the stairs into church on a Saturday afternoon for confession. There, coming down the stairs I met this same fellow, grinning from ear to ear. He had returned to the Church a short time before, and he could hardly contain himself, he was so happy. If I remember right, he said something like, "My mother prayed a long time for me!"

A Disciple's Prayer

Seek the Lord while he may be found,
 call upon him while he is near.
Let the wicked forsake their way,
 and sinners their thoughts;
Let them turn to the Lord to find mercy;
 to our God, who is generous in forgiving. (Isaiah 55:6–7)

11

The Paradox of Knowing God

"For my thoughts are not your thoughts, nor are your ways my ways—oracle of the LORD. *For as the heavens are higher than the earth, so are my ways higher than your ways, my thoughts higher than your thoughts." (Isaiah 55:8–9)*

"I no longer call you slaves, because a slave does not know what his master is doing. I have called you friends, because I have told you everything I have heard from my Father." (John 15:15)

Christianity is full of paradoxes, and these two Scriptures illustrate one of the biggest. On the one hand, as Isaiah tells us, God is far, far beyond our understanding. Both his thoughts and ways of acting vastly exceed our reach. On the other hand, as Jesus makes clear, we are able to draw near to God, hear him, and know him—so close that, like the vine and its branches (see John 15:5), the same sap runs through both him and us. Thus, we become intimate and close to one who is far beyond our understanding.

Something that helped me begin to understand this paradox is the concept of "miscibility" that comes from chemistry. This means that two liquids can be completely mixed in any proportion. When a few drops of water are added to the wine in preparation for the Eucharist, the water disappears into the wine, never to separate again. I think this must be what God had in mind when he created mankind "in his image and likeness." God and man may be very different beings, yet they are "miscible" in some sense. There can be a complete mixing of the two—God into man, man into God. The sap from the vine is the Holy Spirit that flows into us through the sacraments, in prayer, and by our efforts to please God. This is a spiritual reality, but there are also physical realities: God the Son, the Second Person of the Trinity, became Jesus, fully human. Likewise, when we receive the Eucharist, the Body and Blood of

13

Jesus enters and becomes part of us, another form of sap from the vine.

God and man are very different, just as water and wine are very different liquids, but that is no obstacle. We mix—and we become changed in the process—because we are compatible (miscible). Love, that deep and complete sharing of self, is the primary characteristic of God, so it would seem entirely within his nature to share himself with us. Part of the lesson here is that love trumps understanding. Whether with God or the other significant persons in our life, our understanding may be miniscule, but that scarcely matters—it is love that binds us together.

God does not change as he enters us. However, we change; how can we help but be transformed by God's presence within us—Spirit, flesh, and blood? Here is the reality and joy of the Christian life! The Spirit is the foretaste, the first installment, of our heavenly home (see Ephesians 1:13–14; 2 Corinthians 5:5). It is always our choice, but if we consistently desire it, ask for it, and strive to be obedient to his guidance, the Spirit will steadily grow within us. We will transition from believing in God to knowing him. We will come to understand his plan for us—our place in his family, and above all, his love for us. That is joy, and it is real!

Your Daily Life

 The Good News, the Gospel, is very real. In your own life, it may not seem real at this time, but that is just an indication that you have further to travel on your spiritual journey. Be assured that God is always very active in your life; it is only your perception of his activity that is missing, and that will come along later. It doesn't matter where you are now or what your spiritual condition is; no matter how bad, there is still a way for you to experience God's love. Seeking that path and being obedient are the keys. You have to find it on God's terms but find it you can—and find it you will when you seek it persistently.

A Disciple's Prayer

Lord Jesus, I recall your words concerning the Holy Spirit: "And I tell you, ask and you will receive; seek and you will find; knock and the door will be opened to you. For everyone who asks, receives; and the one who seeks, finds; and to the one who knocks, the door will be opened" (Luke 11:9–10). Please, Lord, give me faith in this word and, with that, a still, peaceful heart that I may clearly perceive the whispers of your Spirit.

Creation and Covenant

The Lord created human beings from the earth, and makes them return to earth again. A limited number of days he gave them, but granted them authority over everything on earth. He endowed them with strength like his own, and made them in his image. (Sirach 17:1–3)

Looking down from space, the astronaut can take in at a glance the vast panorama of his homeland, Earth. He sees little of the works of the inhabitants, none of the beauties of flowers or the majesty of wild animals. But, like a traveler looking at a map, he does see the big picture, the relationships in location between cities, roads, and geography, the orientation of major features. Later, when our traveler comes face-to-face with the details, this big picture experience will help him to avoid confusion and appreciate what he sees.

As we begin our discussion of God's plan of salvation, it seems appropriate to start with one of these bird's eye—or traveler's eye, if you will—views of the relationship between God and mankind. Over the centuries, generations of people have walked in that relationship and come to a great deal of understanding. Initially it came by God's revelation, then by appreciation and personal experience, then teaching, more revelation, more experience . . . slowly it accumulated and expanded. The process is not yet complete. In life, and even in the reflections that follow, we will encounter mysteries, areas where our understanding is only partial, and "details," experiences of life which are confusing and unsettling. However, if we can keep in mind the bigger picture of our relationship with God, it will help us with these experiences and our relationship with God will grow.

Our vehicle for this bird's eye view will be the Bible, in particular Sirach 17:1–23. We'll begin with Creation and the verses quoted above, and then continue to work step-by-step through the passage, pointing out the key points as we go.

The first three verses in chapter 17 make at least three important points. First, God created us; we totally owe our existence to him. From other Scriptures—Isaiah 49:5 and Jeremiah 1:5, for instance—we see that this is not merely referring to the general creation of mankind; it is also about the unique, special creation of each one of us. Clearly this implies that we owe God great respect; he quite literally "owns us." Next we see one of the many paradoxes in God's revelation: humans are both very limited (our lives are short), but also very powerful. God granted us authority over everything on earth and gave us a strength "like his own." This speaks volumes about the importance and meaning of each person, of each human life. Finally, we are created in "his image," in the divine image. This implies not only a likeness, but also a very deep and personal compatibility between us and God. Thus the Son, the Second Person of the Trinity, was able to become Jesus, the man, fully human. And now, because of Jesus' saving work, each of us is able to become an adopted child of God, a friend (see John 15:14–15), a member of his household, and able to receive the indwelling of the Holy Spirit. It is hard to bend one's mind around an idea that profound, but in living the experience, it turns out, it is much easier to grasp.

He put fear of them in all flesh, and gave them dominion over beasts and birds. Discernment, tongues, and eyes, ears, and a mind for thinking he gave them. With knowledge and understanding he filled them; good and evil he showed them. He put fear of him into their hearts to show them the grandeur of his works, that they might describe the wonders of his deeds and praise his holy name. (Sirach 17:4–8)

These passages expand the strengths, virtues, and responsibilities of humanity. Particularly important is the knowledge and understanding of good and evil; when we sin, "I didn't know" is not going to get us very far with God. Also important is the duty to describe (proclaim) his deeds and praise his name. God calls us to do all we can to draw everyone toward a right relationship with him, to help everyone know who he is and what he does. As you read verse 8, are you beginning to get some sense of the immense gap between God and man in terms of power, goodness, wisdom and understanding? As Isaiah 55:9 puts it: "For as the heavens are higher than the earth, so are my ways higher than your ways, my thoughts higher than your thoughts."

He set before them knowledge, and allotted to them the law of life. An everlasting covenant he made with them, and his commandments he revealed to them. His majestic glory their eyes beheld, his glorious voice their ears heard. He said to them, "Avoid all evil"; to each of them he gave precepts about their neighbor. Their ways are ever known to him, they cannot be hidden from his eyes. (Sirach 17:9–15)

These verses introduce the covenant God made with mankind. A covenant is similar to a contract, but much more serious. Rather than specific guarantees as you would find in a contract, a covenant is an agreement sealed by the personhood of the parties themselves—their personal dignity, their honor, their very lives. You buy a house or car with a contract; you get married or baptized with a covenant. God has bound himself by his covenants, so we know he is always faithful, always to be trusted. Since this passage is from the Old Testament, the reference is primarily to the covenant made with Moses and the people at Sinai (see Exodus 19:1–15) with its emphasis on keeping the law and avoiding sin. Later, with Jesus, this covenant is fulfilled, continued, and expanded to include openness to all people via Baptism. The emphasis shifts with the New Covenant to its focus on self-sacrificing love, the importance of the community (the Church), our personal relationship with God, and being Jesus' disciples.

Over every nation he appointed a ruler, but Israel is the Lord's own portion. All their works are clear as the sun to him, and his eyes are ever upon their ways. Their iniquities cannot be hidden from him; all their sins are before the Lord.

Human goodness is like a signet ring with God, and virtue he keeps like the apple of his eye. Later he will rise up and repay them, requiting each one as they deserve. (Sirach 17:16–23)

In these final verses we see foreshadowing of the New Covenant, particularly the personal interest God shows for each person. He personally rules the Church (the new Israel), and he is attentive to each and every one of us. We see both his love and appreciation for human goodness and his sense of justice.

Your Daily Life

 The relationship between God and mankind is not a simple thing, and in a very real sense it is unique to each person. However, if you keep these fundamentals in mind, you will find that they go a long way toward sorting out the difficulties and confusion we all invariably encounter as we grow in our relationship with God. Remember, the world will work hard to convince you that God is not there or not interested, that you and what you do are not important—none of that is true!

A Disciple's Prayer

"And I tell you, ask and you will receive; seek and you will find; knock and the door will be opened to you. For everyone who asks, receives; and the one who seeks, finds; and to the one who knocks, the door will be opened." (Luke 11:9–10)

Eucharist and the Mass

Jesus said to them, "Amen, amen, I say to you, unless you eat the flesh of the Son of Man and drink his blood, you do not have life within you. Whoever eats my flesh and drinks my blood has eternal life, and I will raise him on the last day. For my flesh is true food, and my blood is true drink. Whoever eats my flesh and drinks my blood remains in me and I in him. Just as the living Father sent me and I have life because of the Father, so also the one who feeds on me will have life because of me. This is the bread that came down from heaven. Unlike your ancestors who ate and still died, whoever eats this bread will live forever." (John 6:53–58)

Volumes have been written, and more can and should be written about the Eucharist—the Body and Blood of Jesus himself made present and available to the Church. That is why the Church calls it "the source and summit of the Christian life." The focus of this book, however, is our perception of the roles of the Holy Spirit—and in particular his "street level," day-to-day action in the Christian life. Therefore, in this chapter we'll limit our remarks to a few of the more important points about Eucharist, those that bear most heavily on our topic. Of course, it is by the action of the Holy Spirit that priests are ordained and the Eucharist is consecrated—we at least want to say that much. But let's turn now to Eucharist in our day-to-day walk as Christians.

If I had to choose a single word to describe the role of the Eucharist in the Christian life, it would be *home*. Think of what home means in your life:

- Home is your base of operation, the place where you are most often found.
- Home is where you are with your family.
- Home is where you are fed and nourished, both physically with food and intellectually by interactions with family and friends and by the things you do.

21

- Home is where you find rest.
- Home is your shelter, your safe haven.
- Home is where you are healed.
- Home is where you belong, where you know you are loved.

The Eucharist, especially if we include both the Mass and times of adoration of the Blessed Sacrament, clearly embraces all these aspects of life. Eucharist is our spiritual home. It is our base of operation; by attending regularly we become part of the community of believers, members joined with our spiritual family. The food is both physical (tangible) and spiritual (Jesus); the nourishment is real and sustaining. The Scripture, homily, and prayers during Mass nourish both our intellect and spirit.

One common complaint about the Mass is: "I don't get anything out of it." This betrays a very basic misunderstanding about the Christian life. When we think of home, we don't think of "getting something"—at least not something very remarkable or exciting. Home provides peace, rest, nourishment—all that bland but very necessary stuff. More typically, we "get stuff" and experience notable events while we are out, at school or work or on the ball field or wherever.

 I see the same dynamic in the Christian life, especially for people who are young in their faith, who haven't yet developed a two-way communication with the Holy Spirit. The most important thing such people get out of Mass is the proof—to themselves, to the community, and most importantly, to God—that they have chosen to follow Jesus and they know where their spiritual home is and who their family is. When you demonstrate your faithfulness in that manner, God will not fail to demonstrate his faithfulness to you. The gifts of the Holy Spirit, those deepest desires of your heart, will come to you—perhaps not at Mass but because you were at Mass.

I first noticed this when I was still in college. I was a member of the Newman Club, a paltry little group that mostly just used some space in a building next to the church across the street from campus. One day while several of us were chatting, we started adding up the number of couples who met at the club and later got married. We were amazed to realize that the number was around thirty.

A couple of years later, I added to that number. During coffee and donuts after Mass, milling through a crowd of fellow students, my attention was caught by the fire-green eyes of one young lady. To me, her eyes looked like emeralds perfectly lit in a jewelry store. We chatted, I asked her out to breakfast, she accepted, and the rest is history; we have been very happily married for over forty-five years.

Odd circumstances had brought her to that event. She was not Catholic at the time and had never been there before, and she had missed breakfast. Moreover, in all these many years living together, I have never seen her eyes look like that again, not even close. That's as grand a gift as a man can receive, and it's clear to me that God was the giver.

Your Daily Life

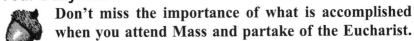 **Don't miss the importance of what is accomplished when you attend Mass and partake of the Eucharist. Each time you attend, you strengthen the parish community, encourage other believers, and witness to its importance in your life. To all who see you, you are similar to the shepherd who walks out in front of the sheep, showing the way. You mark out the path that leads to the truth.**

A Disciple's Prayer

Dear Lord, help me to remember that life is not about me. It is about you and your deep love for each of us. Help me to trust in you, wait with patience for your blessing, and pay sharp attention for your command or guidance. Allow me a place at your table among those who serve you.

Daddy's Children

As proof that you are children, God sent the spirit of his Son into our hearts, crying out, "Abba, Father!" (Galatians 4:6)

Throughout the history of our country, a number of presidents have had children living with them while they served in the White House. John F. Kennedy especially comes to mind; his children, Caroline and John-John, were both very young while he was in office. Such children deserve, and generally receive, the special respect and deference of the country. They are the president's children—a position that bestows a unique honor, but also comes with expectations and constraints on their lives. This is a proper facet of civilized society, a matter of justice and simple respect. It comes from a recognition of the price such people pay in service to the country.

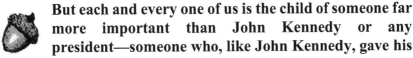 **But each and every one of us is the child of someone far more important than John Kennedy or any president—someone who, like John Kennedy, gave his life for us. Each of us is a child of God, the Creator and Master of everything! Each person, Christian or not, is a unique product of God's creative will (see Jeremiah 1:5) and made in God's likeness (see Genesis 1:26). By Jesus' life, death, and resurrection, the Gift of the Holy Spirit was poured out at Pentecost, making it possible for each person to enter into God's family. Now the Spirit of God now can dwell within each of us, and we can grow into a direct, very personal relationship with him. The respect and deference that was given to Caroline and John-John is owed to every human being, and in a much greater measure.**

This human dignity is a gift of God. It has nothing to do with a person's skills, intelligence, beauty, health, wealth, social standing, religion—none of that. Non-Christians may not be "in the family," but they are still invited to the enjoy the same relationship with God that we have; the door is always open to them. Jesus taught that everybody is our neighbor; as Christians, there is to be no "we" and "them" in how we treat people. Treating others (all others) as you would like to be treated is the bedrock of Christian moral theology.

Your Daily Life

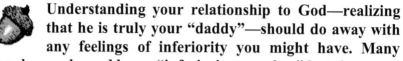**Understanding your relationship to God—realizing that he is truly your "daddy"—should do away with any feelings of inferiority you might have. Many people are plagued by an "inferiority complex," but since each person is uniquely designed and built for a special place in God's creation, feeling inferior makes no sense. It would be the equivalent of saying that one snowflake is better than another!**

In one sense, inadequacy is common to all human beings; we all find ourselves in situations where we are inadequate to cope. On the other hand, many times we also find ourselves not only able to cope but to excel. Inadequacy and excellence provide a window to the mystery and wisdom of God's plan. We all need the help of others, and others need us just as well. We need to practice our Christianity, and the other guy needs to practice his. A spiritual problem encountered with amazing frequency is people who are busy "being Christian," helping others and intent on doing it all themselves. They are more than happy to give help, but never to receive help. I guess they don't realize they are denying others opportunities to practice their Christianity. Serving others is good; helping others in their spiritual growth is much better. There is no need to be jealous of your place in God's family and being prideful is sinful. If you have a ministry, one of your first responsibilities is to train others to replace you; otherwise, the ministry won't be able to continue after God moves you on to something else. So remember, whether you come up inadequate or excel magnificently in a given situation, you never need to feel inferior, or superior, or essential, or not needed. You are loved, unique, and always have a place in the family of God.

A Disciple's Prayer

LORD, show me your way; lead me on a level path because of my enemies.

I believe I shall see the LORD's goodness in the land of the living.

Wait for the LORD, take courage; be stouthearted, wait for the LORD!

Psalm 27:11,13–14)

Supernatural Realities—A Bridge Too Far?

For the kingdom of God is not a matter of talk but of power.
1Corinthians 4:20

Our secular American society applies a lot of pressure to keep us from talking openly about God and religion, especially about a personal and active God. It's not surprising—secularism and religion directly oppose each other. A good example of how effective this pressure is what happens when you are up in front of a class teaching eighth graders. I find all too many of those "that will be the day" blank stares when the topic turns to their prayers being answered or anything else supernatural that might personally involve them. Christianity, and Judaism before that, have several thousand years of experience to the contrary, but our students— and often we ourselves—find it easier to believe the more tangible testimony of daily life.

Clearly this secular strategy is very successful. Sherry Weddell's[4] analysis of Pew Research results shows that only 40 percent of Catholics eighteen to twenty-nine years of age believe it is possible to have a personal relationship with God, and the numbers are not a lot better for other age groups. Perhaps some of you reading this book don't believe such a personal relationship is possible! Not good, considering we are speaking of one of the most fundamental truths of the New Covenant. Therefore, in an effort to keep you from tossing this book in the nearest trash can, let's take a short diversion to relate just one of my personal experiences which illustrate how God has worked in my life. Then at least you have one firsthand testimony, and I'll share some more as we go along.

Many years ago, I was at a conference in the Notre Dame University basketball arena, sitting well up in the back of a crowd of about five thousand people. The speaker was John Wimber, a

---

[4] Sherry A. Weddell, *Forming Intentional Disciples, The Path to Knowing and Following Jesus* (Huntington, Ind.:Our Sunday Visitor, 2012) 45.

29

non-denominational evangelist who was teaching on how to pray for healing. His advice was simple: ask the person what they want prayer for; pause in silent prayer, listening for whatever direction the Holy Spirit might give you; make sure you and the person who wants prayer are agreed on how you should pray; then pray. Next Wimber said he felt that the Lord wanted us to pray for people with back and joint problems, so he invited anyone in the crowd with those issues to stand; the people around them would pray for them as he had just directed.

A little old lady a few feet from me stood up; I noticed that she was equipped with a pair of those crutches which clip to your forearm to help stabilize her balance. I asked what she wanted prayer for, and she said her knees. She was a nurse, and she told me it was very hard for her to make beds and care for people. I listened for the Spirit, and he gave me the thought that I should pray for her shoulder. Discussing that with the lady, she said no, it was definitely her knees that needed healing, but she was OK if I prayed for her shoulder as well. So that's what I did.

A while later in the session, the lady passed me on her way to take a break. On her way back, she stopped and whispered to me, "That's the first time in years that I have been able to walk without pain in my knees." Halleluiah! But that wasn't all. At the end of the session, as people were getting up to leave, she caught me one more time. She said, "I didn't think about it because it never gave me any pain, but years ago I was in an auto accident, and I lost the mobility of my right shoulder." She told me since then she could never lift her arm higher than that shoulder. "But now, look!" she said, and she quickly raised her arm over her head, fully upright.

Events as dramatic as this happen occasionally. I have encountered a fair number over the years, and certainly you will too if you keep watching. What usually comes first, however, and what this book is intended to help you with, is spiritual growth that brings the more subtle guidance and awareness of God's daily work in your life. As

we will see, that is God's intent for a routine, normal Christian life.

Your Daily Life

If you struggle with the idea that the supernatural is real, that God is real, and that he is at work in your life, then ask in prayer to see his works. God loves that prayer. Ask him to reveal his love for you. If you perceive his works and his love, you can follow him much more easily. Obeying God's teaching and the moral law is following him in the general sense, but for a child to follow his father, he must at least see his footsteps.

A Disciple's Prayer

Dear Lord, thank you for being my heavenly Father. I long to see you at work in my life. Please give me an awareness of your deep love for me.

Ruts and Fundamentals

Spiritual concepts, learned while living in a secular environment, too long repeated and rubbed against similar secular ideas, often lose their punch. Like ruts in an old road, people often follow them, but they don't get very far because they miss the key spiritual truths. Here are some meditations, with ruts carefully flagged, on the primary elements of God's plan of salvation and how you fit in.

God Loves You, Right?

For God so loved the world that he gave his only Son, so that everyone who believes in him might not perish but might have eternal life. (John 3:16)

How do you know that God loves you?

John 3:16 is the textbook answer, and it's a good one. The name *Jesus* means "savior" or "healer," and that identifies his mission. Jesus came, died on the cross, and rose again to forgive our sins. He sends us the Holy Spirit to make us part of his family, guide our paths, and make us sharers in the divine life.

That is a great answer for your brain, but what about your heart? How does your heart know you are loved? My guess is that the answer is different for each person. A neighbor child, a rambunctious and rather clumsy little boy, was always falling and taking the hardest knocks. After each fall, his mother would walk over and give him a quick inspection and say, "You're OK," and then return to whatever she was doing. That seemed to be all he needed; he would immediately stop crying and return to his play. Perhaps that provides part of the answer—maybe God just gives some of us the "hard love" we need.

I recall two separate stories of girls who were badly abused when they were young. One girl said to her eight-year-old friend, "Teach me how to pray." Her friend simply told her to find a comfortable rock by the stream near her house and then sit there quietly and talk to God. In the other case, crying alone in her room after being beaten by her father, the little girl would often see a man outside her window, and this vision was somehow comforting. Eventually she figured out it was Jesus. Years later, both girls turned out to be strong and beautiful women of God.

In my own life, I have a very long list of times when God showed me his love. A few were pretty dramatic, like the time early one

April morning in 2011 when my daughter was packing up the kids in the car, about to drop the oldest at school and the toddler at our house so she could go on to work. This was her daily routine, as it had been for a long time. However, this time she had a sense, a feeling that she needed to bring the dogs along and leave them at our house too—something she had never done. Later that afternoon when she came to our house to pick up her daughter, the city was under a tornado warning. Because the dogs were safe at our house, we were able to convince her to delay her drive home with the children. It was a hard sell, as she is not easily swayed from her path, but she delayed and thereby missed being caught in the strong tornado that missed the city but crossed between our house and hers. Three hundred people lost their lives that day, but my daughter's sensitivity to the Spirit kept her and our grandchildren from being added to that number.

In 2019 I related this story to my eighth grade CCD class. As I finished, my co-teacher said, "You know, the same thing happened to me that day." She had been planning to go to the store when her husband came home from work. When the time came, however, she felt uneasy about going, and encouraged by her husband, she decided to stay home. Fifteen minutes later the store where she would have been was flattened by that same tornado! **Note that both my daughter and co-teacher are faithful Catholics, but neither were involved with the Charismatic Renewal. God's love and the soft voice of the Spirit are there for all of us; we simply need to be aware and sensitive to this truth.**

As much as these dramatic events make a good witness, often the times when God gently tickles the innermost strings of your heart give a stronger sense of his love, and they last longer. Little things that only God can do and only you know show you how special you are to him.

I have always loved folk music, and I think a lot about it because it speaks of the people and land and history. For several years a song about life in northern California, one of my favorites, bugged me because it spoke of a place called Pacheco, and I couldn't find it on any map or on the internet. I had lived near northern California and knew the country, but Pacheco alluded, and that really bugged me. Then once I was asked to be Confirmation sponsor for one of my nephews, and I flew out to California for the ceremony. The plane landed in San Jose, and then I drove down to Fresno. Somehow, the trip seemed especially pleasant.

Taking the short but scenic route, my drive took me south, then east across the coastal range on a small, twisting, narrow mountain road. Suddenly, coming around a turn to the top of the pass, a little sign appeared before me. It simply read "Pacheco Canyon." The canyon was small, maybe an hour's drive down, but it was beautiful. At first I figured that God was rewarding me for making the effort to support my nephew, but now I think that he just sent me there to enjoy that little canyon. No words can describe it, but God touched my heart.

 If you don't worry about pleasing yourself, God will do it for you, and he does a really good job.

Your Daily Life

Let me conclude this meditation with a personal observation. It may not be a general truth, but I have seen enough cases that I'm confident it is a frequent occurrence. It seems that people who have a perpetual sense of "not belonging," of not being part of their family or not being loved, even as loving as their environment may be, are also people who have not been baptized. I guess that should not be a surprise. The whole point of Baptism is to end the separation between God and each of us, to establish our belonging to God's family, his adopted sons and daughters. The *Catechism* says that Baptism enables the baptized "to believe in God, to hope in him, and to love him through the theological virtues" (*CCC*,1266). It also says, "Baptism constitutes the foundation of communion among all Christians" (*CCC*, 1271). No wonder it is an effective remedy for this particular type of human emotional and intellectual malady.

A Disciple's Prayer

"Let us know, let us strive to know the Lord; as certain as the dawn is his coming. He will come to us like the rain, like spring rain that waters the earth." (Hosea 6:3)

The New Covenant—Something Overlooked?

For those who are led by the Spirit of God are children of God. For you did not receive a spirit of slavery to fall back into fear, but you received a spirit of adoption, through which we cry, "Abba Father!" The Spirit itself bears witness with our spirit that we are children of God, and if children, then heirs, heirs of God and joint heirs with Christ, if only we suffer with him so that we may also be glorified with him. (Romans 8:14–17)

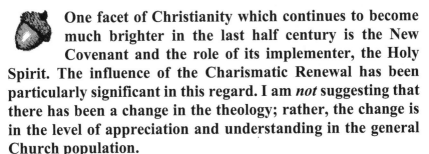 One facet of Christianity which continues to become much brighter in the last half century is the New Covenant and the role of its implementer, the Holy Spirit. The influence of the Charismatic Renewal has been particularly significant in this regard. I am *not* suggesting that there has been a change in the theology; rather, the change is in the level of appreciation and understanding in the general Church population.

The New Covenant is the answer to the question: Why did God send his son, Jesus, to become man, die on the cross and resurrect from the dead? Many of us would answer, following John 3:16, that he came to bring forgiveness and make reparation for our sins and to open the way to eternal life. Interestingly, however, when John the Baptist was addressing that same question, he gave a very different answer. "He will baptize you with the holy spirit and fire" (Matthew 3:11). What was the Baptist getting at? He was addressing the New Covenant, the relationship between God and mankind that Jesus was about to establish. That new relationship is the mechanism by which each of us becomes connected to the forgiveness of sins, the healing, the salvation that Jesus' death and resurrection made possible.

John the Baptist was aware of this prophecy from Jeremiah 31:33–34:

"But this is the covenant I will make with the house of Israel after those days—oracle of the LORD. I will place my law within them, and write it upon their hearts; I will be their God, and they shall be my people. They will no longer teach their friends and relatives, "Know the LORD!" Everyone, from least to greatest, shall know me—oracle of the LORD— for I will forgive their iniquity and no longer remember their sin."

The Church initiates this relationship with the Holy Spirit at Baptism and affirms and strengthens it at Confirmation. These, and all the sacraments, strengthen the action and the presence of the Holy Spirit within you. However, this is not simply a cookie-cutter or one-step operation. Besides the minimum graces assured by the Church, with each sacrament God is likely to give additional graces tailored to your individual needs, your mission, and the "fertile ground" that you offer (see *CCC*,1153). In fact, God's graces are also bestowed in response to prayer, as his will or his love dictate. Christianity offers a lifelong spiritual growth process in which we become increasingly aware of God's love, presence, and power in our lives. The pace of growth is dependent on God's will, God's plan, but also on our faithfulness and willingness.

God said in the Book of Jeremiah, "I will place my law within them, and write it upon their hearts; I will be their God, and they shall be my people" (Jeremiah 31:33–34). John the Baptist announced that Jesus would baptize (soak) us in the Holy Spirit (see Matthew 3:5). Jesus himself affirms it (see John 14:26) and tells us that he himself will abide in us (see John 15:26). St. Paul writes about it in his letters; the verses from Romans 8 quoted above expands on the same point. The New Covenant is a brand-new type of relationship with God the Father, God the Son, and God the Holy Spirit—the entire Trinity! This incredible relationship is offered to us freely, but we must seek it, ask for, accept it, and grow into it by our own free choice.

At this point we note that understanding of the New Covenant really only comes by experience, in the living-out of the relationship. The witnesses, discussion of the gifts of the Spirit, baptism in the Spirit, and other topics which form the rest of this book will show you what to look for and some of the blessings you can expect.

 We conclude this reflection with a summary of the five most important points, points which form the structural support of the whole:

1. **The New Covenant is what links us to the life, death, and resurrection of Jesus, all of his saving work. Its primary implementation is in the Church.**

2. **The New Covenant is a relationship of love, a covenant of the heart. We must choose to love and express that choice in daily prayer, asking God to conform our heart to his. This allows the Holy Spirit to transform us; he will not do it without our permission. When we ask the Holy Spirit to enter and transform our lives, he will do it. Slowly or quickly (one never knows), we will be baptized (immersed) in God's Spirit. Asking is a crucial secret of spiritual growth.**

3. **Our relationship with God is meant to be one of communion. Communication becomes real. We no longer just believe in God; we *know* God. This relationship becomes very deep and very personal. We are, in fact, sharing in the divine nature (see 2 Peter 1:4; *CCC*, 460). Consider the Mass and the real presence of Christ in the Eucharist. Consider also the indwelling of the Holy Spirit, which is given to us at Baptism and increases with Confirmation and the other sacraments. Sharing in the divine nature includes every aspect of life—physical, intellectual, spiritual—and it brings freedom and joy!**

4. **The New Covenant is a family relationship. We are sons and daughters by adoption, but adoption makes us full members of God's household, not second-class citizens. As such we are expected to embrace both the duties and**

the benefits of membership in the family. In essence, we are now part of a "family business"—we have a purpose, a special mission we are called to. Jesus came to heal, save, relieve suffering, and lovingly help others. Those are the tasks of the Master and thus the work of everybody in this household. Only the details differ according to the Lord's will for each of us.

5. The New Covenant, besides being deep and personal, is a social, community-based relationship. It does not function well, if at all, without this dimension. Covenant means family, and there is room in this household for everybody.

A Disciple's Prayer

Praying the Psalms is an excellent, time proven form of prayer. Pick a psalm of your choosing, prayerfully recite a few verses, and then add your own thoughts. Here is an example:

> To you I raise my eyes,
>   to you enthroned in heaven.
> Yes, like the eyes of servants
>   on the hand of their masters,
> Like the eyes of a maid
>   on the hand of her mistress,
> So our eyes are on the LORD our God,
>   till we are shown favor. (Psalm 123:1–2)

Holy Spirit, increase your presence in my life. Show me how I may be at home with you and serve you well.

Believe

"Do you not believe that I am in the Father and the Father is in me?" (John 14:10)

Following Jesus Christ has great significance; it impacts every facet of your life probably more than you realize. Beginning with a prayer every morning, your relationship with Jesus should influence every decision, every priority, and every moral issue throughout the day. And yet, in this skeptical, "scientific," high-tech world, many of us, especially young adults, question why they should believe the ancient revelations and accounts found in the Bible and Church teaching. Let's begin with a look at the development of faith, and then we'll take a further look at what to believe and why:

The Transition from Belief to Faith

Belief and faith are not exactly the same thing. Belief is an intellectual assent to the facts. A belief may or may not exert a strong influence on your decisions.[5] Faith, on the other hand, is a gift—you can't generate it within yourself. It comes by hearing the Word of God and by God working gently in our lives, often barely detected. Faith, if it is strong, always has an influence on what you do. Christian spiritual growth begins with the process of belief growing into faith.

So where do we begin?

Answer Number 1 (partial): Logic and reason are always available to help you; they supplement the other answers which follow. Never check your brain at the door! Especially when emotions are involved, reason may lead you to wait and to go slow until the picture clarifies.

---

[5] We are speaking of "belief" in the modern American sense of the term. In Israel at the time of Jesus, "belief" always implied actions would accompany it.

Answer Number 2 (provisional): Often you are asked to accept something as true simply because somebody says it's true. You need to make a decision, so you take the best information available and move forward—provisionally. Your confidence, or lack of confidence, in the source of the information is a primary factor to consider. In these cases, you should always keep in mind that something may be wrong, incomplete, or tainted. Parents, teachers, friends, history, and education all play a big role in providing guidance, and reason can help us decide where to place our confidence. For example, Christianity has grown and has been followed seriously by millions of people for about two thousand years now. That's a strong indication that it contains something of value; it may not be perfect—it isn't—but staying with the program is a reasonable choice.

Answer Number 3 (best): Scripture, of all the sources that support Answer Number 2, is by far the best attested, especially when it is considered as a whole, not on a line-by-line basis. Scripture itself teaches us to judge things by the fruit they bear (see Matthew 7:15–20, for example), and that is generally the best you can do. You move forward based on provisional understanding, but with time you see the fruit of your decisions. Good fruit—love, joy, peace, patience, and so on (see Galatians 5:22)—confirms a good choice, while poor fruit indicates that a change is needed. Be patient, reflect on your behavior, and be honest with yourself, and you'll start to see your faith grow.

Answer Number 4 (even better yet, in a sense): A fundamental teaching, one of the truths of Christianity, is that God offers us a direct and personal relationship with him, and in that relationship, he guides us to the truth. In that relationship you "recognize his voice," and the spiritual gifts of wisdom and understanding and prophesy come into play. You still rely on Answer Number 3 for evaluating the correctness of a decision—you can't do better than that—but new dimensions of knowing the truth and growth in faith itself open up based on your direct relationship with God. This dynamic is particularly important in the middle of a conversation or other "on the fly" situations. When you hear God's voice, respond as he indicates, then witness the good fruit it bears. This is a typical pattern for using the New Testament gifts of the Spirit (see 1 Corinthians 12), and with practice, both belief and faith become grounded on experience. More to come on this subject.

Science and Reasons to Believe

Before we move on to discussion of our personal relationship with God and the spiritual gifts, let's look at some additional reasons for belief. The search for God, for Christianity, is always the result of a call on the heart, but that call must also be supported by reason, and these ideas may help in that regard. In the end, your faith will not rest on these truths, but these may help get you there.

1. It is the only reasonable thing to do. The famous scientist Blaise Pascal (1623–1662), besides contributing important work in geometry, mathematics, probability theory, and atmospheric pressure, also gave us a theological argument that has become known as Pascal's Wager. In his book *Pensées*, he pointed out, "If God does not exist, one will lose nothing by believing in him, while if he does exist, one will lose everything by not believing." In other words, when the odds are anywhere near even, the cost of placing the bet is small, and the payoff very large in comparison (such as eternal life), it is foolish not to place the bet.

2. There are compelling classical arguments that prove God exists. In addition to Pascal's Wager, people find these classical arguments compelling when they are open to believing in God, and not so compelling if they would rather not. There is a principle hidden here: God always honors our free will. These proofs are easily available in any book on Christian apologetics, so we will not treat them in detail here.[6] The line of reasoning typically goes like this: anything you observe has a cause, that cause had a cause, and so on back to

---

[6] I recommend Peter Kreeft's *Fundamentals of the Faith* for an easy read.

the beginning; that beginning had to be God, the un-caused cause. You can switch to other realities and follow the same logic, moving from observation to the necessity of a source (i.e., a reason) for the observation. Since there are physical laws and moral laws, there must be a law giver; since there is design in nature, there must be a designer; since there are miracles, there must be a miracle worker.

3. Science does not address the general philosophical question of why. Science is tied to observations (i.e., data) of the physical world, and it uses reason and mathematics to project and explain a sequence of events, that which has been observed and will be observed next. Take gravity, for instance: any two physical bodies attract each other in proportion to their masses and the inverse of the distance between them. The mathematics is very precise and describes precisely what will happen as the bodies interact, but it says nothing about why. What is it that causes the attraction? Physicists have thought long and hard about this question, debating "action at a distance" and "gravitational fields," and then later "curvature of space." The description of what happens is very accurate, but science cannot effectively address the question of why it is that way.

4. The fact that science is limited by its tie to physical observations has other important implications. God is not physical (the Eucharist excepted); he is spiritual and most of his work is in the spiritual realm. Likewise, humans have intellect and free will. Both humans and God are creative. That's why science has no data, except miracles (i.e., observations science cannot explain) for addressing questions such as why creation is the way it is, why we should believe in God, or how to define beauty, or skill, or wisdom. Science predicts truth only in a very limited domain. There is a word for the idea that science proves there is no God or that we don't need him—that word is *deception* or, at best, *speculation*. Science without data is not science.

Your Daily Life

There are at least two important lessons to be drawn from this reflection on faith and belief. First, belief in God is the rational choice, especially as an initial position. It is the choice that is compatible with the good things in life and draws one toward love, joy, peace, patience, kindness, generosity, faithfulness, gentleness, and self-control. Notice also that the goal of Christianity is to bring these good things to everybody, not just a few individuals. This is not true of the popular trends in secular morality, where we will always find winners and losers. Abortion is the most obvious example, but it is true for the rest as well.

The second lesson is the need for patience. God's love for each of us is intense, but in no way does he wish to push, bully, or coerce us. It certainly might be easier to believe in him if he were more forceful, but then it would be much more difficult to truly love him in return. Remember, God is seeking a relationship with you that lasts more than a lifetime! Seek him the way he seeks you.

A Disciple's Prayer

Hear my voice, LORD, when I call;
  have mercy on me and answer me.
Even if my father and mother forsake me,
  the LORD will take me in.
I believe I shall see the LORD's goodness
  in the land of the living.
Wait for the LORD, take courage;
  be stouthearted, wait for the LORD!
(Selected verses from Psalm 27)

Baptism, Sonship, and Focus

But when the fullness of time had come, God sent his Son, born of a woman, born under the law, to ransom those under the law, so that we might receive adoption. As proof that you are children, God sent the spirit of his Son into our hearts, crying out, "Abba, Father!" So you are no longer a slave but a child, and if a child then also an heir, through God. (Galatians 4:4–7)

This passage from Galatians refers to sacramental Baptism, but in the context of spiritual growth we must expand the reference to Confirmation (see Romans 8:14–17; *CCC*, 1303) and also to the many other channels the Lord uses to send the graces of the Holy Spirit upon us. By virtue of Jesus' life, death, and resurrection, the Spirit comes upon us and lives in us, indelibly adopting us as children of God, his beloved sons and daughters, members of his household. It is the greatest of gifts, freely given. The *Catechism* clearly affirms this relationship between Baptism, the Holy Spirit freely given, and adoption as sons and daughters of God (see *CCC*, 1213, 1265, 1216).

It is impossible to overemphasize the importance of this point—after all, it provides the focal point of the Christian life and spiritual growth. Knowing that we are his adopted children defines our relationship to God, our roles, our goals, our spiritual authority, our responsibilities, our needs, our resources—the list goes on and on. Our adoption as God's children and the resulting relationship with the Holy Spirit is the covenant Jesus established by his salvific work. It is the whole point of Christianity. And yet all too often this point seems to be lost in teachings about the role of the Holy Spirit in the Church.

For example, very frequently presentations focus almost exclusively on the Spirit's gifts as enumerated in Isaiah 11, or perhaps on his role as sanctifier. Rarely are the broad and creative manifestations that bring life to the entire Church highlighted. The Holy Spirit's roles of sanctifier, consoler, and fortifier are important, but this is hardly the whole story. An idea of the scope is perhaps better indicated by *Iuvenescit Ecclesia* ("The Church Rejuvenates") by the Congregation for the Doctrine of the Faith. This letter points out that the life-giving, charismatic gifts freely distributed by the Holy Spirit are "co-essential" to the mission of the Church along with the hierarchical gifts (i.e., the gifts conferred through ordination).

Many of us don't fully appreciate or clearly understand the relationship between the Spirit and our status as adopted children of God. Often so much emphasis is placed on repentance and avoiding sin (sanctification) that the positive demands of our adoption by God are not adequately appreciated. Adoption and sanctification all come together at Baptism. Adoption, our status as God's sons or daughters, is the indelible mark of the sacrament (*CCC*, 1272). As sons and daughters of God, we have the power to live and act in accord with the promptings of the Holy Spirit—this is discipleship and mission—as well as to grow in goodness and moral virtues (see *CCC*, 1266). These two aspects work together. Can you see here Jesus' teaching on how those who are faithful in small things will be given greater responsibilities? Baptism matured confers upon us the ability (and responsibility) to regain a state of grace (after sin), grow in sanctification, and participate in the mission of the Church.

In the Parable of the Prodigal Son (see Luke 15:11–32), Jesus tells the story of two young men who are not in a good relationship with their father. The younger son, impatient with the work and being obedient to the father, demands and is given his inheritance. He leaves home, squanders the inheritance, and then, realizing the error of his ways, returns home, hoping only to be able to live as a slave in his father's house. His father, full of love, accepts him back with open arms. The youth has lost his inheritance but not his sonship. His sonship has drawn him back to his salvation. The parallel is clear for us. When we sin—when we fail to fulfill the obedience required of us as members of God's household—we are in danger of forfeiting our inheritance (including eternal life), but we always have the option of repenting (turning back) and being received again by our Father.

The eldest son, on the other hand, patiently endures the demands of the work and obeys his father, but he fails to claim his inheritance. He chooses to serve as a slave, not accepting the role or the authority and privileges of the adult son and eventual master of the plantation. Rather than a loving kinship with his father, he resents his situation. As an adult member of the household, he has the privilege and responsibility of sharing in the planning, goals, and vision of the household. The same is true for us. As we mature in our Christianity, we too are called to embrace the goals and vision of the kingdom of God. We are called to embrace our roles as disciples of Christ, and as we do, we shall also be blessed by the gifts and the fruits of the Spirit. After all, Jesus promises, "My yoke is easy, and my burden light" (Matthew 11:30).

Your Daily Life

Priorities are important in all aspects of life, and the spiritual life is no exception. The implications of your status as an adopted child in God's household should lead you to focus on the positive aspects of Christianity and all that it means to be a disciple of Christ. Positively focusing on the Beatitudes[7] and the works of mercy (both corporal and spiritual) will provide you each day with something you can do to further the work of God's household and spread the fruit of the Spirit to those around you. Of course you'll strive to avoid actions that hurt God's plans (sin), but this is a "negative goal"—an impediment to be avoided. To bear the most fruit, your focus should always be on the positive. You can think of it as a football team that has a goal of winning games. To reach their goal, team members must exercise discipline and avoid fouls

---

[7] Matthew 5:2-12

51

resulting in penalties that forfeit the yards gained. But overall, their coach will put the emphasis on the positive goal: winning.

A Disciple's Prayer

Lord, make me a channel of your peace and a responsive servant of your Word. Open my eyes and heart so I may clearly know my place in your household, know that I am loved, and serve your family well.

Daily Discipleship

Then he said to all, "If anyone wishes to come after me, he must deny himself and take up his cross daily and follow me. For whoever wishes to save his life will lose it, but whoever loses his life for my sake will save it. What profit is there for one to gain the whole world yet lose or forfeit himself?" (Luke 9:23–25)

Blaise Pascal wrote, "Small minds are concerned with the extraordinary, great minds with the ordinary." Keep this useful bit of wisdom in mind when you read the above passage (or very similar passages in Luke 14:27; 17:33; Matthew 16:24–28; 10:38; Mark 8:34–38; 9:1). The crucifixion of Jesus was not only an extraordinary event, it was emotionally gripping as well. As you read the word *cross*, preceded by *deny himself* and followed by *loses his life*, suddenly the passage seems difficult to understand and even harder to swallow. Without diminishing the extraordinary aspects in any way, let me explain how the word *daily* led me to a practical understanding for more ordinary days.

The subheading for this passage is typically something like "Conditions of Discipleship." Christianity always calls us to follow in the footsteps of Jesus; Jesus is the model for our lives. The cross was the focal point of his ministry. Jesus taught, healed, forgave sins, and instilled hope, faith, and love, but his ministry always came down to that final critical sequence of events: dying on the cross, rising again, ascending into heaven, and finally sending the Holy Spirit—all of which makes it possible for us to follow him.

One day as I was pondering this passage, I had an insight. It is right there in that subheading. What this Scripture says is not that God wants our daily suffering; rather, God wants *daily discipleship*. He wants us to be faithful to our calling, our ministry, our mission. We can expect to experience some pain, heartbreak, and suffering; we are, after all, dealing with the human condition. We should also expect persecutions (see Matthew 10:16–42; Mark 10:29–30). And yet, there are also many blessings, protections, and compensations. When reflecting on these verses from Luke, Matthew or Mark, also keep in mind Matthew 11:30, "For my yoke is easy and my burden light"!

In the end, this is all about the immense significance of God's personal call and the seriousness of the ministry he entrusts to each individual. Like a good master sergeant training his troops, Jesus carefully prepares us, emphasizing both the importance of the work and the severity of the difficulties to be expected. This is no child's game. The building of God's kingdom and the salvation of many souls is at stake.

Here we encounter something of a paradox. Nothing could be more serious than the call to discipleship; it is true, this is no child's game. **However, in living out this call, just the opposite is true. It is very much a child's game in that children are almost totally dependent on its parents and other adults to care for them. The success of our discipleship depends primarily on God and on the guidance and action of the Holy Spirit. For our part, we first must be willing, and then we must become men and women of prayer so we are able to perceive the guidance of the Holy Spirit.** To say it another way, first we must make the decision and then we must put in the time; these are both within our human reach. There are more elements that contribute—faith, holiness, and the fruit of the Holy Spirit— but these elements are the products of our spiritual growth, the work of God within us. Whenever we make some small effort at discipleship—such as reaching out to pray with someone, to comfort or encourage someone, or to witness to our faith, God has the opportunity to minister to the person and get the credit, and the Holy Spirit will be sure that we grow from the experience.

Here we have focused on "ordinary," day-to-day discipleship, but there is one more very important point we need to make clear: *ordinary* in no way implies that it is not supernatural or somehow independent of God's intervention. Indeed, only with the intervention of Jesus and the Holy Spirit can good fruit be borne. "Apart from me you can do nothing" (John 15:5). All of Jesus' ministry was done in response to and in coordination with the Father and, by implication, the Holy Spirit. If we are to be his disciples, we also must work by that same method. Like Jesus, we are sons and daughters of that same Father. It's not that our natural or human efforts are of no value, but to be fully disciples, we must work with the spiritual gifts.

Your Daily Life

Living as a disciple of Jesus is God's call to all Christians, all people; it is central to the New Covenant. Following Baptism, the Sacrament of Confirmation opens a door to the flow of graces that gradually leads to Christian maturity and the opportunity to be effective disciples of the Lord. Of course, you must walk through that door, keeping the ground fertile (maintaining a holy environment) and as free of weeds (sin) as possible. Discipleship is perhaps most important when choosing your occupation or other facets of your path in life. Vocations to the priesthood or religious life are prime examples of Christian discipleship. However, they are only examples. All occupations are a matter for discernment and should be in accord with the call to discipleship. That call applies equally to everyone. If you discern that God is calling you to lay bricks, then lay bricks. That's where your lamp will shine brightest: helping others, healing others, and drawing others to salvation.

A Disciple's Prayer

Loving Father, give me courage that I may not be overly concerned what others think of me or what difficulties may lie before me. Rather, let me stand as a strong servant of your Son, always faithful and attentive to the leadings of your Spirit. Yes, come, Holy Spirit, come!

Spiritual Gifts

Do you not believe that I am in the Father and the Father is in me? The words that I speak to you I do not speak on my own. The Father who dwells in me is doing his works. Believe me that I am in the Father and the Father is in me, or else, believe because of the works themselves. Amen, amen, I say to you, whoever believes in me will do the works that I do, and will do greater ones than these, because I am going to the Father. And whatever you ask in my name, I will do, so that the Father may be glorified in the Son. If you ask anything of me in my name, I will do it. (John 14:10–14)

Everything God has done for us—sending Jesus, our salvation and forgiveness of sins, the sacraments, etc.—it is all fundamentally gift. Christianity is a gift. God's gifts are, or at least should be, part of the normal routine for all Christians. The gifts of the Holy Spirit form an important subset of this bigger picture; these gifts are expressions of God's power that we are meant to experience during our day-to-day Christian life.

There are two primary listings of the gifts of the Spirit in Scripture, but these are neither independent nor complete; what the Holy Spirit decides to do to express God's love is not restricted by any list. The first list is found in the eleventh chapter of the Book of Isaiah: wisdom, understanding, counsel (right judgment), knowledge, fortitude (courage), piety (reverence), and fear of the Lord (wonder and awe). Notice that these are primarily gifts you would associate with spiritual maturity. The second list is from the New Testament and is found in 1 Corinthians 12:8–11[8]— expression of wisdom, expression of knowledge, faith, healing, mighty deeds, prophecy, discernment of spirits, varieties of tongues, and interpretation of tongues. Later in the same chapter, Paul adds, with a focus on the role in the community, apostles, prophets, teachers, gifts of healing, assistance, administration, and

---

[8] Ephesians 4:11-12 and Romans 12:6-8 also give short lists of the gifts.

varieties of tongues. This second list relates to relationships between people, ministry, or, as Paul put it, to building up the Church.

Key Points:

All of these gifts can be said to have natural counterparts, but we'll focus here on the supernatural versions of these abilities. Each one is a unique action of the Holy Spirit working in and through you. For example, "knowledge" is knowledge of a specific fact that could not be known by any natural process.

• With your spiritual growth and growth in your responsibilities, you will frequently use gifts from a "short list," gifts that are needed for your mission, your part in God's plan. You "have" these gifts because your experience brings knowledge, deep understanding, and high confidence (faith) in them. Beyond that, unique situations will occasionally arise where God prompts you to invoke one of the other gifts. For either type of situation, you initiate the operation of the gift by your prayer, or laying on of hands, or speaking out, etc., and the rest is handled by the Holy Spirit.

• While the gifts are supernatural, and you realize that you are cooperating with the Spirit, they do not *feel* "supernatural" or extraordinary. God designed us to live in close relationship with him and to implement his gifts. Think of yourself as a squeegee with a short handle. When a longer handle is needed to do the job, the Holy Spirit just screws in an extension to the handle, but it's still all very routine.

• The gifts of the Spirit are available to all Christians, even children and the newly baptized, so stepping forward based on hope and expressing love is good and bears fruit, even when you don't have a direct sense of God's wishes for the specific situation. But it takes some faith and boldness to do that, which is why the gifts become much more evident and effective after a person is baptized in the Holy Spirit.

- Scripture assures us that God always answers our prayers (see Luke 11:9–13, for example), but there are some caveats. For example, I would not expect a prayer that compromises another person's free will to be answered, at least not directly. Also, having a prayer answered and perceiving the answer are two different things.
- Receiving the gifts, as with the baptism in the Holy Spirit, requires that you want them and that you ask for them. Generally some persistence is required in this matter, but God knows our hearts and acts accordingly.

Your Daily Life

Here we come to a pinch point, the reality of being stuck in a situation where you would really like to use one of the spiritual gifts — observation tells you it is really needed — but you also feel an intense pressure, social pressure, not to step forward and offer the prayer that would bring the gift. After all, think what will happen; people will think you are some kind of religious zealot, and everyone will know. *You will stick out like a sore thumb and no one will want to associate with you* — that is the fear, and the fear and the pressure are very real. Be assured the devil has worked very hard to make sure of that. It even has a name, it is called *fear of man.*

To escape from this pickle in the manner the Lord would wish requires some hope, faith, and courage. Scripture has it right there with the descriptions of discipleship, it is that *laying down one's life* thing. It is not easy to be God's disciple, the first attempts will probably take all the hope, faith and courage you can find or borrow. However, it does get easier, a lot easier, with the doing. For one thing, you will quickly learn that the devil has very little to back up his threats. If in the off chance that he actually has someone to ridicule you, it quickly becomes apparent that they are the one who is the outsider, who no one wants to associate with.

By their very nature, God draws people; the devil isolates them. Beyond that, God does answer prayer, he does work miracles, and he is extremely faithful in support of his disciples.

Beyond all that, remember that the public witness of God's presence and his love is extremely important to him; it is absolutely essential to drawing people into the kingdom, to saving them. Paul makes this point in Romans, chapter 9, going back to Old Testament references. I remember well the struggle I had with fear of man when I was young. Eating in a restaurant, I would quickly bow my head and say the blessings, then the sign of the cross. By avoiding the sign of the cross at the beginning, I figured I would draw less attention. **Even tougher were the times I felt the Lord wanted me to wear a wooden cross, almost four inches long, to work. One trip to the Kennedy Space Center was especially tough, witnessing in front of a dozen strangers. However, several of the Kennedy folks caught me off to the side and complimented me for the witness, and some other good things happened. God not only covets our discipleship, he also trains us in it.**

A Disciple's Prayer
Dear Lord, how often I find myself weak, confused, and in the bondage of fear. What can I do in a world so full of hate, anger, and deception? I will follow the example, and pray the prayer of your servant David, for even when he failed, you were faithful.

In you, LORD, I take refuge;
  let me never be put to shame.
In your righteousness deliver me;
  incline your ear to me;
  make haste to rescue me!
Be my rock of refuge,
  a stronghold to save me.
For you are my rock and my fortress;
  for your name's sake lead me and guide me.
Free me from the net they have set for me,
  for you are my refuge.   Psalm 31:2-5

A Preview of the Gifts

This section provides an introduction to the spiritual gifts, comments on some common misconceptions, and witness to three cases of their operation and the role of mutual support.

Time to Heal

So the words of Tobit's hymn of praise came to an end. Tobit died in peace at the age of a hundred and twelve and was buried with honor in Nineveh. He was fifty-eight years old when he lost his eyesight, and after he recovered it he lived in prosperity, giving alms; he continued to fear God and give thanks to the divine Majesty. (Tobit 14:1–2)

Tobit and Job are two well-known examples of books in Scripture where, in spite of their holiness and dedication to God, God's protagonists struggle long and hard before their prayers are eventually answered and everything works out for the better. Joseph in Egypt, Moses and the Exodus, Paul's missionary journeys, his "thorn in the flesh," and his imprisonment provide other examples. These events in their lives represent years of struggle filled with uncertainty as to how things would work out, before the wisdom and blessing of God's plan became evident to those involved.

These examples of long struggle stand in stark contrast to the many miracles worked by the Old Testament prophets, Jesus, and New Testament apostles. Miracles shine as examples of God's manifest power, direct and immediate proof that God is present, powerful, and in complete charge of the situation. In the face of a miracle, there is no doubt that God loves us; God's kingdom is at hand.

But what about today? When we pray for healing or relief from some struggle of life, when should we expect the answer? Certainly, we'd all prefer miracles every time, not only for quick relief, but also for the assurance of God's love and care. But that is not the question. The question is when *should* we expect our prayer to be answered, not when do we want it answered. In reality, prayer may be answered at any time. **The answer may be immediate, or it may not become apparent for decades, or it may fall somewhere in between. God has promised to answer our prayers, but he has not said when or how; there is always more involved.**

There is no question that God wants to answer your prayer, to heal or to relieve the struggle in which you are engaged. Jesus' very name means "healer" and "savior"—healing and saving is what he is all about. No, he certainly wants to answer your prayer and he will answer it, but that fact does not do away with the complexity involved about how and when. For one thing, God has higher priorities than healing or saving only you; he wants to heal and save all people—as many as possible. Each of us is linked tightly with many other people in society. How God deals with us affects others and has implications on their lives and salvation. There are also implications regarding the free will of all those persons. God's salvation must be the free choice of each of us. How should he answer your prayer and bring the most benefit to all that answer will touch? Is the complexity of the situation starting to become apparent?

Another important factor is human weakness. Is your current struggle or need of healing simply a forewarning of more serious problems to come if you do not repent or take some other path? The issue might be simple, such as the time God showed me that my back pains were the result of the lack of proper stretching and always crossing my legs in the same direction.

Other situations are more serious. I recall one fellow who was confined to a wheelchair in the middle of life; he counted it one of his biggest blessings because he knew he had been heading in a bad direction spiritually before the handicap. My own experience includes something similar. I've mentioned how much I love folk music. If I had had even an ounce of musical talent when I was young, the draw to be a performer would have been irresistible and my path in life much different. Now, decades later, I understand the trouble I would have been in and what I would have lost had I chosen such a path. We serve a God who considers our weaknesses and knows how to steer us to the best, most productive life for each of us.

Yet another factor that can result in significant delays in receiving answers to prayer derives from God's gentleness and his desire to completely restore us. Illness, injuries, and struggles impact our entire lives, not just our daily schedule. They affect how we look at the world, society, life, our emotions, our intellectual understanding, and our understanding of who we really are. (In a similar way, extraordinary beauty or athletic gifts also impact our lives for better or worse.) The more serious the illness or struggle and the longer it has persisted, the more restoration and healing is required. God works to be both gentle and complete in answering our prayers, so it should be no surprise that recovery from deep-seated, long-term issues takes longer than recovery from less serious and more recent problems. And often the most visible aspect of a healing, the physical part, may well be the last to occur.

Hopefully this gives some perspective as to why it may seem to be a long time before a prayer is answered, but what about the opposite case when the response is immediate? God sometimes answers in miraculous fashion to make another point, something above and beyond just answering an isolated prayer. A miracle might confirm the sainthood of a person whose cause is under consideration by the Church. At church conferences and other teaching events, especially those sponsored by the Catholic Charismatic Renewal, miracles frequently occur that affirm the message of a teacher or the conference as a whole. This, of course, is the case of most, if not all, scriptural miracles—God is affirming both Jesus or the prophet or apostle involved and their message.

Your Daily Life

I see two important applications; both relate to discipleship and both apply to many difficult situations, not just healing. First, as disciples of Jesus, we should always be patient and continue to trust in him. Though we can and should pray for healing for ourselves and those we love, we should keep in mind the tougher aspects of discipleship; it demands discipline and self-denial and above all acceptance of God's plan in every circumstance. The operative word is humility.

> "Is he grateful to that servant because he did what was commanded? So should it be with you. When you have done all you have been commanded, say, 'We are unprofitable servants; we have done what we were obliged to do'" (Luke 17:9–10).

The reality is that we are small pawns in a very big game; we should not think too much of ourselves.

Second, given the complexity often found in healing and other difficult situations, we should also keep in mind that a successful resolution may require the application of many spiritual gifts: wisdom, knowledge, understanding, healing, discernment of spirits, deliverance, or inner healing. Moreover, God is a jealous God; he wants the credit; he wants the witness of his love and power. That's why his "plan A" usually always involves the participation of his disciples.

As an example, Catherine Labouré was a simple nun merely trying to do her job well. One night she was obedient to the sense that she should move to the chapel for prayer. Who could foresee the importance of that response, a response that led to the Miraculous Medal and the declaration of the dogma of the Immaculate Conception? In the beginning we might not understand "plan A"; we only understand the gentle prompting in the heart that calls for our response. Do not hesitate—it is the work of the small pawns that is critical to the Lord's work. We are small pawns, true, but we are also witnesses and ambassadors for the Creator of the Universe.

A Disciple's Prayer
Holy Spirit, come again to me today. Help me to hear your voice clearly and to respond with wisdom and courage.

Witness: A Healing

Do not be anxious about anything, but in everything, by prayer and petition, with thanksgiving, present your request to God. And the peace of God, which transcends all understanding, will guard your hearts and your minds in Christ Jesus. (Philippians 4:6–7)

Note: No matter how dark the situation, with God there is always hope. That is the first lesson of Leonore's witness presented here. Beyond that, the unmarked days of sacrifice, discipleship, and prayer make us able to walk in that hope. That is a second lesson we should learn.

Lenore: In July 1991 while we were living in California, I received a phone call from my dad in Indiana. He tried to explain through tears that Mom was in the hospital. She had had surgery in June, and she seemed to have recovered, but her body at age seventy-six was apparently traumatized. A couple weeks later while at the hairdresser's, she felt faint and turned white. Dad immediately rushed her to the ER. After a scan, they positively identified that one of her kidneys had shut down. Thankfully, my employer at the time was very understanding; I was allowed to leave on the next flight to Indiana—a blessing from God.

By the time I arrived at the hospital, Mom was in Intensive Care. I sighed as I gazed at all the life-support tubes coming out of her and how swollen her face was, but I was not startled by these. Within hours, while they were preparing her for another scan, her heart monitor showed an almost straight line. The nurse told me to keep Mom awake at all costs while they contacted the doctor. When I jokingly told my mother I was going to use toothpicks to hold her eyes open, she smiled at me. My dad was standing behind me sobbing. This disturbing scene would have disheartened anyone, and yet I felt God's presence. Consoling my father, I knew that my past experiences were helping me to cope with this moment.

Mom's whole kidney was now in shutdown mode, but she was hanging on.

A number of years prior to Mom's kidney failure, after becoming Eucharistic Ministers, my husband and I felt called to fill the need in our parish of ministering to the sick and infirm. Together we would go to the hospital, when it was still possible to obtain a list of Catholics there. We were part of a larger group of Eucharistic Ministers from several surrounding area churches. We would separate the list according to different sections of the hospital. Dale and I would sometimes have a list of twenty or more on a Sunday morning. We saw people hooked up to multiple tubes. We saw various cancer patients, some with brain cancer with swollen heads who were possibly untreatable. We became familiar with patients who were downtrodden because of their medical situation. We also visited nursing homes and witnessed dementia in the lovely elderly who would smile when they saw us coming. We prayed with them, cried with them, and brought the holiest of holies, Jesus in the sacrament of Communion, to them. Little did we ever think that there would be a time in our own family when we would see some of these same things.

By the grace of God, those previous experiences prepared me for my mom's hospitalization. As I said, seeing the tubes did not startle me, but instead were a sign from God that his mercy endures forever. My mother was a victim of crippling rheumatoid arthritis. She suffered with excruciating pain most of her life, beginning with her eighteenth birthday. I could see the emptiness in Dad's eyes as he sank into a chair. My father did not know the saving power of the Holy Spirit that could heal my mother, nor the fruits that soothe our hearts.

As I collapsed into a chair next to Dad in the waiting room, I slowly raised my eyes and saw an old friend. I knew instantly God had preordained this moment. I hollered so loudly that everyone in the room could hear me. "Jane, Jane, hello there!" I sprang out of my chair and swept my old charismatic friend into my arms tightly, as though I was hugging the Lord himself! Back in 1978, my children and I had lived in my hometown while Dale was stationed in Korea. I had joined the prayer group at St. Mary's Church, and that's when I met Jane and other devoted charismatics I instantaneously loved. Now God had given me Jane to pray with, though she was taken by surprise. It had been nearly fifteen years since we had prayed together weekly, and she was not quite sure she remembered me. Thankfully, after some conversation, Jane did recall who I was.

Jesus says, "Again, [amen,] I say to you, if two of you agree on earth about anything for which they are to pray, it shall be granted to them by my heavenly Father. For where two or three are gathered together in my name, there am I in the midst of them" (Matthew 18:19–20). I knew the Lord had given us this opportunity to pray together for my mom, and we did. We found a quiet area, and Jane began, "Lord, we praise you and thank you for your presence with us in the Holy Spirit. We know that you love Leonore's mother, and that you know about this situation. But Lord, we don't think this is the right time for her to go. She is still needed here. We have confidence in your presence with her. We know that you are the center of her life, and she relinquishes to you her all, but Jesus, will you please give her back to her family? We pray with the Holy Spirit in Jesus' precious name."

That night, Dad and I slept as much as we could, but we got up early to make sure we would be able to speak to the doctor. We waited outside the ICU to be let inside, when suddenly a nurse blasted through the door and yelled, "Mr. Mitchell, Mr. Mitchell, *your wife's kidney kicked in!*" What? Could it be? Obviously God answered our prayers! The doctor in charge could not believe that my mom, at age seventy-six, actually had a revived kidney! I told him I knew exactly why this happened—it was God's loving answer to our heartfelt prayer the day before. That night we propped up Mom and watched the stunning fireworks display from her large window. I stood back a little and simply observed the spectacular view, framed by my mom in the padded chair and my dad looking over her at the Fourth of July sight. Mom lived another ten years, bringing much joy to our lives. "Thanks be to God who gives us the victory through our Lord Jesus Christ" (1 Corinthians 15:57).

Your Daily Life

 The trials and tribulations in your life can be a preparation for the future, so cherish them. As you continue to walk the path of a committed disciple of Jesus, you will come to recognize that the New Testament gifts of the Holy Spirit are real—very real. Your faith and your belief system will be enhanced by using them. Scripture tell us that these gifts are for the common good (see 1 Corinthians 12:7), so they must be a visible witness to God's love and power. This means that someone must be bold, step forward, and lay hands on the person being prayed for or in some other way give visible witness. Confirmation is in part the initiation of your spiritual walk, and there is far to go beyond that point. The Charismatic Renewal has much to teach about the spiritual gifts and many aids to growth in faith.

A Disciple's Prayer

Oh, Holy Spirit, open my eyes and my heart to your powerful gifts. Help me to be a faithful disciple of the Lord Jesus and reveal to me when and how to use your gifts for the good of your people. Keep me always in the household of faith; let my life be a witness to the many fruits of your grace and love.

Wisdom

All wisdom is from the Lord and remains with him
* forever.*
The sands of the sea, the drops of rain, the days of
* eternity—who can count them?*
Heaven's height, earth's extent, the abyss and
* wisdom—who can explore them?*
Before all other things wisdom was created; and
* prudent understanding, from eternity.*
The root of wisdom—to whom has it been
* revealed? Her subtleties—who knows them?*
There is but one, wise and truly awesome, seated
* upon his throne—the Lord.*
It is he who created her, saw her and measured her,
* Poured her forth upon all his works,*
upon every living thing according to his bounty,
* lavished her upon those who love him.*
(Sirach 1:1–10)

One of the principles of Christianity I continue to find interesting is that Christian truths work in all phases of reality: from the natural physical world and the realm of human nature, society, governments, and nations to the spiritual, supernatural realm. A good illustration of this principle is the gift of wisdom. The scriptural poem from Sirach quoted above expresses both the scope and depth of God's wisdom gifts. Wisdom itself comes in ways that span all modes of reality—i.e., there is both natural wisdom and supernatural wisdom. They differ according to the applications as well as the source, but ultimately, they both come from God.

Christ teaches repeatedly that we are not to focus on ourselves; rather, our focus should be outward, toward God and toward our neighbors. In terms of intellectual input, focusing on yourself is like fishing in a bucket—you won't catch much because there just isn't much there to catch. When you focus outward, on the other hand, you have the whole universe to catch; you are constantly exposed to a changing array of people, things, events, and ideas. Wisdom, especially natural wisdom, is certainly a matter of both intellect and temperament, but its growth is fed by the input of experience. Focus your life outward as Jesus directs, and you will have a very large pool—an ocean—from which to catch ideas that nourish wisdom.

Spiritual wisdom is not completely separate from natural wisdom. Rather, think of it as an extension of natural wisdom and don't try to draw too sharp a line between the two. Just the other day, for instance, the phone rang; it was a call from a close friend of ours who was facing a difficult dilemma and seeking prayer and help. My wife was right there with me (and no one else was around), so I put the call on speaker so we could both hear. The matter in question was one that I had had some direct personal experience with, but to tell the truth, I was dumbfounded by the problem. My wife, on the other hand, who heard exactly the same conversation, perceived the situation very differently than I did. She was immediately able to bless and guide our friend with her wisdom. That wisdom was pretty simple and straightforward; I would have said something very similar if—and that's a big if—I had perceived the problem correctly. But I did not perceive it. I was Mr. Blank Brain, actually misled in this case by my experience. But God is good and knows when we need help. The Holy Spirit put together the timing of the call with the availability of the right person—my wife—with the correct perception of the issue. It might seem like a very natural process, and in a sense it is, but it doesn't work without that light touch from God.

Our natural wisdom is a gift from God, given when he designed and built us, and it grows with experience. Likewise, spiritual wisdom grows as we mature as disciples of Christ. God's wisdom is tailored to the mission he plans for us, the work he calls us to do, and the fruit he expects us to bear. We do, after all, have a purpose! As we are faithful in following that call and faithful in using the tools he left for us—the sacraments, prayer, and Scripture reading—we become familiar with his ways. This feeds our ability to perceive reality, first the natural and, as we grow, the spiritual.

As we can see from the little example just given, correct perception of the situation is the first step in wisdom. The second step is perceiving and selecting the appropriate response. This, too, grows with our experience of the Christian life as we come to see and understand the many ways God works. Sadly, there is also another side to this coin: sin clouds our conscience and corrupts the concrete judgment of good and evil (see *CCC*, 1895 and Wisdom 1:4). Thus, wisdom is partially a result of the path we choose.

Your Daily Life

A person can grow in knowledge by study, but spiritual wisdom is a gift from God. Wisdom benefits from experience, but study will not earn it. However, there is an option which is within our grasp: we can take seriously God's call to become disciples of Jesus. Discipleship is a journey that typically begins with small opportunities to serve God. As we prove faithful in these little things, we will be called to greater tasks—tasks that require greater spiritual wisdom. Our discipleship matures into a mission.

Spiritual wisdom, being a gift of the Holy Spirit, comes in response to a prayer for increased guidance from the Holy Spirit. Pray also to see the results, the fruits of your actions; you want to be able to recognize spiritual wisdom in operation. There are many powerful servants of God who don't recognize the gifts operating within them, and as a result they may struggle with discouragement.

A Disciple's Prayer

Though I walk amid distress, you preserve me; against the anger of my enemies you raise your hand;
Your right hand saves me. The Lord will complete what he has done for me;
your kindness, O Lord, endures forever;
Forsake not the work of your hands. (Psalm 138:7–8, NAB)

Witness: School Friends, a Treasure from God

The Advocate, the Holy Spirit that the Father will send in my name –he will teach you everything and remind you of all that I told you. Peace I leave with you; my peace I give to you. Do not let your hearts be troubled or afraid. (John 14:26)

Note: Being a child of God means that we appreciate, like children, the smallest gifts. As Leonore shares, it is the small gifts that enable us to keep God's peace during the hectic pace of modern life. Watch for them and treasure them!

Leonore: Summers in the south were always breathtakingly beautiful, with flowers flourishing in the hot, humid temperatures. We lived in Huntsville, Alabama, where my desires to start back to college again blossomed. Eighteen years earlier, I had to drop out of the second semester of my first year at Indiana University. Infectious mononucleosis . . . that's what the doctor said I had, and I needed to rest or it could affect my health in general. That was the only way to get over it back in 1963, so leaving school was my only alternative.

Later in 1981, married and with two kids of our own, it appeared that my husband would be stationed at Redstone Arsenal in Huntsville for several years, so this was my opportunity to finish my degree. The University of Alabama at Huntsville was about fifteen minutes from our home, and though I was slightly apprehensive, I felt a certain peace about doing this. My neighbor and friend Nancy decided to join me and complete her engineering degree. We were both approaching forty, and believe me, we felt "old" in the company of kids who had just graduated from high school. It sounds silly, but at that time, it was unusual to see students of our age roaming the campus. As we stood in line to register for fall classes, we met Sandra, with whom I found several things in common. Something clicked in my mind. Enlightened by the Spirit of God, I asked myself, "Perhaps these encounters mean that I am following God's will for me?" Somehow, I felt the Holy Spirit nudging me with God's peace.

Our first week at UAH proved to be a learning experience. Walking from one building to another and finding our classrooms was all new to us. One day as I walked to my next class, a young lady smiled at me, and I returned a smile. Once again, I knew that the Lord was smiling at me with his everlasting peace. It was a great revelation! Nancy and I were happy that, given our schedule of classes, we would have enough time each morning to pray at Mass—my lifelong desire. As a kid, I attended a Catholic elementary school which was an hourlong bus ride away, and most of the time I did not arrive early enough to attend the whole Mass before school. I vowed that when I was on my own, I would go to Mass every day. Receiving Jesus in the holy Sacrament of Communion was extremely important to me and always proved to be strengthening. At that school I received the Sacrament of Confirmation, truly a turning point for me. I began consciously looking for God's presence. In the second semester at UAH, as early spring approached, we spotted a budding dogwood tree, one of my favorite flowers. Day after day we watched the buds slowly spread their petals and emit a delicate scent. I plucked a blossom and thought about how it revealed signs of the passing winter and the coming of new life. In a very peaceful way, it meant God was blessing our lives paths with his array of beauty.

Thirty-six years of future blooming dogwoods witnessed many changes in our lives. As Catholics, Nancy and I shared a strong relationship. She and I often prayed together on our way to morning class, while Sandra and I simply "connected." We shared several classes and became study buddies. Sandra was grounded in solid Christian ideals. These two friendships grew over the years, with common denominators of college, family, and our Christian values.

After several moves, Nancy now calls Huntsville her home. She is a grandma like I am, which we both dearly love being. Sandra moved with her husband to Virginia to be closer to their daughter's family. And we moved to Colorado to be close to our son and daughter and their families. The three of us all have had multiple changes in our lives, but one thing always has stayed the same. We all have held firm to our Christian values. When we hear "by their fruits shall we know them," it is so true. We love one another, we are kind and patient with each other, and our faith has not been shaken. The joy of knowing Jesus as our Savior has become our faithful commitment. With the graces and gifts we receive from the Holy Spirit, we continue to grow as followers of Jesus. Wonders at the awe of God have blossomed in each of us. Now in our aged lives, we still hold fast to God the Father and call Jesus our friend. And we feel the gentle breath of the Holy Spirit enfolding us.

Your Daily Life

 Be aware of even the smallest blessing in your life, acknowledging its source is God. Friends are valuable assets, so choose them well. Budding flowers eventually fade and blow in the wind, but God's love for you never ends. Notice the changing seasons of your life. Ask God to send you his Spirit, that you might walk in the light, always trusting Him to lead you on your path of life.

A Disciple's Prayer

Spirit of love and peace, show me the light of your presence. Help me grasp the challenges in my life with confidence by following the will of my Heavenly Father. I embrace the fruits of the Spirit: love, joy, peace, patience, kindness, goodness, faithfulness, gentleness, and self-control.

Finding New Spiritual Depth

Here we begin to dig deeper into our life in relationship to God and our mission as his children. We include an introduction to the baptism in the Holy Spirit and two helpful examples.

Mission

After this the Lord appointed seventy-two others whom he sent ahead of him in pairs to every town and place he intended to visit. He said to them, "The harvest is abundant but the laborers are few; so ask the master of the harvest to send out laborers for his harvest. (Luke 10:1–2)

Mission is a crucial element of the Christian walk, and understanding it requires a look at it from two perspectives: first the general one, the mission of the Church (i.e., all Christians), and second, our personal mission and, in particular, the key question that always seems to pop up, "How do I know what that is?" Luke 10:1–20 will provide the subject of this reflection. We'll recall a few key verses for you as we proceed.

When Jesus established the New Covenant, he also established the mission of that covenant. This mission is not an option; it is essential for all who choose to participate. The mission is described succinctly in several ways in the New Testament. First there is the call, repeated often, to be disciples of Jesus—to follow him and do as he did. Jesus is the way—that is, he is not only our example, but also the means for being his disciples. We cannot follow him as we should without his direct help given to us through the Holy Spirit (see John 15:4–6).

So, what did Jesus do that we should follow? How do you recognize this new work of the kingdom of God? Primarily Jesus healed, not just physical healing, although there were many examples of that, but healing in the broadest sense. He healed mental disorders, casting out demons; he fed the hungry, freed captives (see John 8:1–11), lifted up social outcasts (see Luke 19:1–10), and remedied just about every other kind of human suffering. Jesus also taught us how to live and how to care for one another, so as to avoid much suffering (Matthew 5:3–10 is most notable, but there are many examples

in the Gospels). In his teachings Jesus repeatedly emphasized the importance of faithful, watchful, fruitful servants furthering the kingdom here on earth. Finally, Jesus established his Church and the Eucharist, and then, following his death and resurrection, he sent the Holy Spirit to dwell in each Christian, all of which enables our participation.

It should be clear that healing and revealing the kingdom is not some side point of Jesus' work; rather, it is the central point for him and for us as well. Let's look at the example of Luke 10 and pull this into better focus:

• The seventy-two are sent into every town and place. The immediate situation was limited to the localities Jesus himself intended to visit, but the implication is clear from the total Christian message as well as the comments about asking for more laborers for the harvest: for us the mission is the entire world, every town and place, period.

• "I am sending you like lambs among wolves" (Luke 10:3, see also verses 17–20). Yes, there will be very real opposition; the image of Jesus himself being sent to the cross comes quickly to mind, as do the martyrs and wild beasts in the Colosseum in Rome. However, Jesus also walked through and away from the angry crowd at Nazareth that was intent on casting him off a hill (see Luke 4:29–30), Peter walked out of jail one night, freed by an angel (see Acts 5:19), and Paul, bitten by a viper, simply shook it off into the fire and suffered no harm (see Acts 28:3–6). There are many examples of suffering because of the mission as well as many other examples of believers having the power "to tread upon serpents" and escape all harm. Understanding comes with the realization that death has no power—not over Jesus and not over his disciples. It's not a question of luck—actually, luck does not exist; everything is in God's hands.

• "Carry no money bag, no sack, no sandals; and greet no one along the way" (Luke 10:4). The mission is of absolute, paramount importance to God, and it should be the same to us. We are to make no provision for ourselves and we must not get distracted. This self-denial is certainly, at least on paper, the most difficult aspect of the Christian message. It only makes sense when we look at the big picture with eyes of faith; then God reveals the light of his love and grace, and spiritual growth is the result. By growth and grace, God's mission becomes our mission, so the logical conflict disappears. We will come to see God's interests as our own interests. And, also by growth and grace, God's love becomes a matter of experience. God is more than willing to give us any good gift we need or want as long as it does not present an obstacle to our role in his work. God can and does meet our every need. When you look back at your life and see a long list of blessings mixed with times disaster was avoided (no thanks to you), then your confidence grows that his plan is better than yours even when you understand so little.

• "First say, 'Peace to this household' . . . cure the sick in it and say to them, 'The kingdom of God is at hand for you.'" (Luke 10:5–9). **Some people wonder:** *Why should I follow God? Why be concerned with religion when there is so much violence, hunger, disease, and suffering in the world?* **However, healing and preventing violence, hunger, disease, and suffering is exactly God's mission, and thus the mission of Christianity. These distressful situations are characteristic of the world, not of the kingdom of God, where peace and joy reign—now imperfectly, later perfectly.**

As we turn to focus on finding your personal mission, there are a few additional important points that deserve emphasis. First, bringing about the kingdom is primarily God's work; it comes by his initiative and grace. Our role is supporting this work; but while it is limited, that role is still essential. Did you ever try carpentry without a hammer? Try anything without the proper tools? Did you ever receive a note but not know the messenger or sender? It leaves you perplexed, right? The same is true of God's work: we are only God's tools, the point where the hammer hits the nail, and his messengers, yet we are critical to accomplishing the task.

Next, think again about the great diversity and scope of God's mission. Think also of the great diversity of human struggles—intellectual, emotional, political, environmental, and social—from violent eruptions visible to all down to silent interior struggles known only to the sufferer and God. All things are to be brought under submission to God. Whatever, wherever the disorder, God's intent is to heal it, restore good order, and prevent another occurrence. The point is simply that all aspects of human life are involved. Whatever a person's status, occupation, or role in life, he or she is in just the right place to contribute to God's work.

 So, how does one identify his or her mission? The short answer is: Take a prayerful look back. What have you done that has borne good fruit in your life? A careful look at the Beatitudes[9] and virtues will help in this. Even more helpful, ask God in prayer to show you the fruit you have produced. In short, identify where God has used you and build on that. Many people don't even think of mission is the sense we are using it here, but the light of their Christian virtue shines far and wide—a blessing upon them!

There is much more to be said about the subject of mission, and the discussion on the baptism in the Holy Spirit which follows in the next chapter should help a lot. baptism in the Spirit is about direct communication with God and the New Testament gifts of the Spirit. It increases our zeal to serve the Lord, so our question about mission becomes more significant. We will return to this discussion in several of the reflections which follow, but for now just know that the Holy Spirit's action in our lives often seems very natural and mundane, just another everyday occurrence. You may be moving mountains and not even be aware of it.

---

[9] Matthew 5:2-12

Your Daily Life

Holiness and the kingdom of God are, in a very basic sense, beyond human reach. They are gifts that come from God with our cooperation. Your mission is part of that cooperation, and it is not out of human reach. Your mission is the work you were designed and built to do. It starts by trusting God and loving your fellow man. It starts with prayer and being attentive to the needs of those around you. Mission is the handle you are offered, a handle you can reach— grab it and hold on with all your strength. It will not only bear fruit, it will serve to increase your holiness and draw you deeper into the kingdom. If it slips from your hand, grab it again.

A Disciple's Prayer

Dear Lord, I want to accept your mission. I know that there are things for me to do in this world, tasks that will help further your kingdom. Open my eyes and ears that I may better perceive your guidance. Help me to do all that you command me to do!

The Baptism in the Holy Spirit

"I have come to set the earth on fire, and how I wish it were already blazing! There is a baptism with which I must be baptized, and how great is my anguish until it is accomplished. (Luke 12:49–50)

I think one needs to be cautious when pondering the meaning of these two verses in Luke 12. It seems pretty obvious that Jesus is talking about his baptism in his own blood—his death on the cross and subsequent resurrection—which will open salvation and forgiveness of sin to all those who believe. Right? Certainly. Amen!

So where is the cause for caution? It lies, I would suggest, in that last word, *Amen.* "Amen" is not in the Scripture quoted, but it is a natural human reaction. Jesus' death and resurrection was a powerful, gripping event. Like an earthquake or tornado, it was so dramatic that it grabs all our attention. All other considerations easily drop from our minds. Here it would be all too easy to lose focus on what Jesus was so anxious to accomplish, his purpose: "to set the earth on fire." John the Baptist says it clearly: "He will baptize you with the Holy Spirit and with fire" (Matthew 3:11; see Luke 3:16). Likewise, in John's Last Supper narrative, it is clear Jesus is thinking about what will follow his death and resurrection: the arrival of the Holy Spirit. In John 14:12, Jesus says, "Amen, amen, I say to you, whoever believes in me will do the works that I do, and will do greater ones than these, because I am going to the Father." Jesus is looking forward to Pentecost, when the Holy Spirit is given to the New Covenant community of believers—the Spirit who, with the community, sets the earth on fire.

So what exactly is the baptism in the Holy Spirit and what does it mean for today's Church in today's society? The baptism in the Holy Spirit is perhaps best thought of as a threshold in the process of spiritual growth, a benchmark in our awareness of the presence and grace of the

Holy Spirit. However, it is more than that, it is a grace unique to each person and thus unique to the times and situation in which each person lives.

In what might be called the normal path of a Christian life, the indwelling of the Spirit occurs at Baptism and comes with an indelible mark (character), adoption into God's family, and the forgiveness of sin. With the Sacrament of Eucharist, we are strengthened and changed by the indwelling of Jesus himself. At Confirmation the Church prays for the Gift of the Holy Spirit to be bestowed and for further strengthening and growth in the relationship between God and the individual. As each person's faith and commitment allow, the fruits of the Spirit grow within their life. However, throughout this process the rate of spiritual growth is modulated, strengthened or inhibited by the person's free will, interest, and choices.

Baptism in the Holy Spirit is different, yet it is part of the same process. It comes as a gift from Jesus only when he sees the heart is ready. Sometimes it comes as the result of prayer, and sometimes it comes out of the blue along life's path. I have seen it happen to non-Christians before being baptized as well as to serious, mature Christians. Often it comes in response to the prayer of others already baptized in the Spirit. And while God is generous with the gift of his Spirit and all people are "eligible" to receive it (see Luke 11:9–13), it is clear that God picks the time and place. Only God knows when a person's faith, commitment, and circumstances are right. I recall the testimony of one priest who prayed earnestly for this gift but did not receive it until three years later. Why the wait? I don't think he ever found out.

 Perhaps the most striking aspect of being baptized in the Spirit is the fact that a person knows, without a doubt, that they have it. It is experiential but also lasting. As St. Paul put it, "For our gospel did not come to you in word alone, but also in power and in the holy Spirit and [with] much conviction" (1 Thessalonians 1:5). Before, you may believe in God, believe that a personal relationship with God is possible, even believe (correctly) that you have such a relationship. After being baptized in the Spirit, *believe* no longer applies. It seems silly to use that word. You *know*, the way you know your spouse or child. You know you are loved, a disciple of Jesus, and your life is focused on that relationship.

There is one other thing you quickly come to know: walking in the light of Christ is really, really good. No wonder Scripture characterizes the presence of the Holy Spirit as the foretaste of heaven (see Ephesians 1:13–14; 2 Corinthians 5:5). Yes, life still has its struggles and problems, but somehow the texture of life has changed. I can't say that fear, doubt, anger, and similar spiritual impediments disappear, but somehow they are diminished and no longer an intrinsic part of you. Gently the Spirit works to heal and remove such problems. Life is still full of struggles and obstacles, but somehow, for you, the Spirit has coated the sharp edges with a protective film; they cannot cut so deep. One often hears people in the Charismatic Renewal say, "I don't see how people can live without the Spirit!"

 Another key aspect of the baptism in the Holy Spirit is that it brings a zeal to draw others to Christ, and with that it also brings new tools, the charismatic gifts (see 1 Corinthians 12), to help in that endeavor. It quickly becomes apparent that it is the Holy Spirit doing the evangelizing, not us. We are servants supporting the process. Here is a short example from my own experience: Once I found myself in a discussion over some point of Christianity with my neighbors who attended a very fundamentalist Protestant church. It wasn't an argument; it was very friendly, but we did disagree. In the middle of the conversation, the Spirit gave me a word of knowledge, a Scripture chapter and verse from one of the letters to the Corinthians. I had no idea what it said, but I said to my neighbor, "Well, what about [here I quoted the reference]? One of us picked up a Bible, looked it up, and the discussion ended right there. The passage made my point perfectly. There was another funny result of this—a few weeks later these same neighbors brought their minister by to meet us. They said they had never met Catholics who knew their Bible before. I just chuckled inside—it was the Spirit who knew the Bible!

In the preparation process for the Sacrament of Confirmation, the Church places a strong emphasis on the gifts of the Spirit listed in Isaiah 11; wisdom, understanding, counsel, piety, fortitude, knowledge, and fear of the Lord. Notice that these gifts are all important in bringing a person to Christian maturity, and thus the emphasis here is well placed. Lasting fruit for the kingdom of God comes with maturity, and people receiving Confirmation are usually young in their spiritual walk. However, there are many other spiritual gifts discussed in Scripture that the Lord provides, sometimes in response to a particular situation, but also regularly to persons in support of their ministry. Similarly, priests and deacons are anointed with gifts in support of their sacramental and pastoral duties.

Once a person (either lay or ordained) receives the baptism in the Spirit, there will be an additional flowering and outpouring of spiritual gifts, especially those found in 1 Corinthians 12, Ephesians 4, and Romans 12 in support of the person's growth into the mission to which they are called. Note that while the baptism in the Spirit is a unique event (i.e., a transition into a new quality of relationship with God), the sending of the gifts is not. The Spirit bestows gifts both before and after receiving the sacraments and before and after baptism in the Spirit; the difference is in number, frequency, permanence, magnitude, and so on. Continual prayer for the coming of the Spirit and the outpouring of the spiritual gifts should be a focal point of everyone's Christian walk. In preparation for Confirmation, this should be made clear; additional gifts are yet to come, they are essential to bearing good fruit for God, and they need to be invited by prayer.

Finally, it should be emphasized that while being baptized in the Spirit is always a highlight of the Christian walk, it is not the culmination of it. Spiritual growth begins before this event and continues for the rest of one's life. From a general, historical point of view, since Pentecost, the baptism in the Spirit has always been with the Church, especially in the lives of the saints. However, with the "New Pentecost" that started showing up in non-denominational communities in the early 1900s and gave rise to the Catholic Charismatic Renewal in February 1967, baptism in the Spirit has spread in unprecedented power and numbers. Since its beginning, the Church has increasingly approved and encouraged the Renewal. Pope Francis has called for the baptism in the Holy Spirit to be spread to the entire Church, as noted at the beginning of this book. The Charismatic Renewal is spiritually linked to the New Evangelization and efforts to increase unity within Christianity. Truly, this is an era of amazing grace for the Church.

Receiving Baptism in the Holy Spirit
If you are wondering whether you have already crossed the baptism in the Holy Spirit threshold, then the answer is almost certainly no, not yet. There might be some question in the initial days after you receive it, but that soon fades, and you know without a doubt you have it.

Perhaps my own experience would be a good illustration. It was 1972 and the Renewal was very new. I was twenty-eight years old, and my wife and I were visiting my brother and his wife. They lived eighty miles from us, so we only saw them occasionally. They had been involved with the Renewal for a year or so, and the Lord had given them a nudge that they should pray for us to receive the "gifts of the Spirit." Anyway, after a very short explanation, probably not more than five minutes, I remember thinking, *Well, if it's from God, I don't want to turn him down, and if it isn't, nothing will happen.* So I let my brother and his wife pray for me, and they prayed for my wife too. Immediately after that we got up and hit the road for home, wondering if anything had happened.

In the days that immediately followed, however, I started noticing the difference. I had a desire to read Scripture, and it became alive for me; I also spoke a couple words in an unknown tongue. My wife also noticed a subtle change.

A few months later, we went to hear a Catholic abbot with a gift of healing speak; again, my brother and sister-in-law were with us. After his talk we lined up for individual prayer. Actually, I was only there to support my sister-in-law, but I wasn't standing very close to her. When the abbot came to me and ask what I wanted prayer for, he caught me totally off guard. I mumbled, "More faith," the only thing I could think of. He prayed briefly for me and then moved on to the next person.

My brother and his wife left for home immediately after the meeting, and I didn't see them again for a couple months. The next time we were at their house, I asked for an antacid; I was having a lot of stomach trouble from the stress of facing my doctorial comprehensive exams. My sister-in-law answered, "This morning in my prayer time, the Lord seemed to tell me that you could have been healed when the abbot prayed for you, but instead you asked for more faith. Is that right?" Well, that certainly built my faith— it had to be God, or at least one of his angels. No other explanation was possible. The increase in faith also did wonders for my stress level.

Your Daily Life

 The dramatic outpouring of the baptism in the Holy Spirit and the Catholic Charismatic Renewal is still very new to the Church, being just over fifty years old. Thus, there is still much to be learned and much questioning within both Church and society in general. Much of God's plan is still unclear, but certainly this is a time of rapid change and great grace for the people of God. My goal in writing this book is to help clarify these events and illustrate not only their power and meaning, but their ties to traditional aspects of Catholicism, especially to the Sacraments, as well as their links to the most fundamental truths of Christian thought.

For more information about these topics, an excellent source is the book, *Baptism in the Holy Spirit*, published by an international Catholic charismatic renewal doctrinal commission in 2012. In the United States it can be ordered from Pentecost Today, USA ☽

https://www.pentecosttodayusa.org or 800.338.2445. They also maintain listings of other useful books and local organizations within the Renewal, if you would like to make contact with a local prayer group.

A Disciple's Prayer

Holy Spirit, come to me. Open my mind and heart that I may receive you and your gifts worthily. Help me to be your useful and faithful servant.

Witness: Fear Not

For you did not receive a spirit of slavery to fall back into fear, but you received a spirit of adoption, through which we cry, "Abba, Father!" (Romans 8:15)

For all of us, but especially for teens and folks in their early twenties, the idea of always being told what to do is repugnant. When I was that age, I was not happy about the possibility of being drafted into the army. I was also not open to the constraints associated with the priesthood. For this reason Jesus' call to discipleship with its requirement that each of us "must deny himself and take up his cross daily and follow me" becomes a tough nut to swallow, especially for young people.

There is, however, a very good answer which relieves this fear. Perhaps Bishop Robert Barron put it best in one of his video chats: Such fears are totally reasonable if we are talking about such authority over our lives imposed by another person. Any of us would object, and rightly so. However, we are not giving that authority to just another human person; we are giving it to God, the God who formed us and who loves us. That is a very different situation. God knows what we need and desire, and he knows the future and how to guide us through it. In short, he knows what will please us the most and how to provide it. He wants us free and happy and fulfilled.

Accepting Jesus' lordship does not mean giving up the desires of your heart, although the path may be quite different than you would expect. For one, God has designed and built you for the career path he desires for you. He has given you many of the skills and interests you need to be successful and enjoy your career. Yes, God works with us in the natural as well as the supernatural.

Once I heard a priest talking about how to find your ministry within a parish. He said you first look for work you are passionate about. When you put in long hours, go home sick and tired of it, but then rise again the next day ready to tackle the problems one more time, you know you have found your mission.

The idea that I should become a scientist goes back so far, at least to middle school, that I have long forgotten what triggered it. Most good scientists seem to develop an interest in one particular science, and their curiosity about that topic drives them. I was different; all through high school, college, and even the first two years of graduate study, one science seemed as good as another to me. One of George Gamow's books about the International Geophysical Year and the suspense of the early space program certainly contributed to my interest in physics, but in reality, I chose physics because it seemed most likely to keep my options open.

Finally, when I was looking for a topic to begin my doctorial work, Professor John Hallett caught me in the hallway and asked if I would be interested in working with him. He had funding and I needed a summer job, so I agreed on the spot to work over the summer with him, and to stay if I liked it. Cloud physics was interesting and practical, and John was an excellent mentor. The rest is history. The cloud physics group was working on a project with NASA, so a year after I finished my degree, I was able to get a NASA position at a time when almost no jobs were available anywhere.

Looking back, God kept me on a direct path to where he wanted me, even though I could see none of it. Psalm 16:5–6 describes it well: "LORD, my allotted portion and my cup, you have made my destiny secure. Pleasant places were measured out for me; fair to me indeed is my inheritance." My Christianity was not mature in those days, so I wasn't thinking, *What does God want?* Rather, it was more of a vague *What should I do?* Later in this book, Leonore's "Witness: Trust in the Lord," gives us another example involving more mature folks.

Your Daily Life

The lesson here is very simple; always trust in God and follow him. Fear not. The path might involve years of frustration, hard work, or even suffering but you will be able to manage fine, and in the end it is worth every minute and every drop of sweat. Looking back on the process not only is God's love very real, but also your immense value to him and the intrinsic value of who you are.

A Disciple's Prayer

Lord, help me to not fear and not hesitate to follow you. Help me to remember your promise and my place in your family: "For you did not receive a spirit of slavery to fall back into fear, but you received a spirit of adoption, through which we cry, 'Abba, Father!'" (Romans 8:15).

The Passing of the Law

The law and the prophets lasted until John; but from then on the kingdom of God is proclaimed, and everyone who enters does so with violence. It is easier for heaven and earth to pass away than for the smallest part of a letter of the law to become invalid. (Luke 16:16–17)

Here we find a puzzle. In this passage from Luke, "the Law" refers to the Torah—the first five books of the Hebrew Scriptures, what we call the Old Testament. Jesus made it clear that the coming of the kingdom of God does not abolish even the least part of the Law; rather, it fulfills it (see Matthew 5:17). So if one is passing from the domain of the Mosaic Law into the domain of the Law fulfilled, where does this "violence" come from? Why are "people of every sort forcing their way in" (to quote the 1971 edition of the NAB)? Is the conflict between the Law and the Law fulfilled? Bible scholars throughout the years have agreed that these verses are "very difficult."

 There is a sharp discrepancy between the Mosaic Law as understood by the Jews of Jesus' time and the kingdom Jesus proclaimed. The discrepancy is not in content as much as in priority and authority. Where does the ultimate authority lie? The Jews considered themselves "People of the Book" and the book, the Law given by God through Moses, was considered the ultimate authority. This perspective is very different than what Jesus proclaimed. In his kingdom Jesus himself is the ultimate authority. Always in harmony with the Father and ever alive and present to his people by the action of the Holy Spirit, Jesus is Lord and Master. The Law may not have lost a jot or tittle, but its place in religious thinking now, rather than being the pinnacle of belief and understanding, is more like the steps to the temple— it guides and protects those who would enter until their relationship in the family of God is fully established. It remains ever present and essential, but it is no longer the focus of the

spiritual life. Christianity is not a religion "of the book." Rather, it is a religion of the living Word of God, Jesus (see CCC, 108).

Here we have plenty of reason for violence to arise—first, in the sense of the kingdom being assaulted. When the ultimate authority of a culture is called into question and begins to be displaced by another, it is not surprising that conflict will arise between the two groups as it did between Jews and Christians in the first century. Then as now, "the book" is essential, trustworthy, central to the foundation of Christianity as it is for the Jews, but it does not stand alone as the ultimate authority of Christian belief.

Another form of violence we see is of a very different sort. It is the violence of self-struggle, of self-discipline and growth in faith as we enter ever more deeply into a direct and personal relationship with God. The Law may be difficult to follow—after all, we all sin—but it is relatively clear, relatively concrete, relatively precise. Believing in the Law, we can be quite comfortable with knowing what is expected of us. According to the Law, God is a personal God; he sets up a direct relationship between himself and the Israelite people (see Exodus 19—23). However, this relationship is between God and the community, not between God and the individual in the same sense as it is in the New Covenant established by Jesus.

 In the New Testament sense, the relationship with God is more personal, more open-ended, more mysterious, and more uncertain as to what is likely to be required. It is a relationship between the individual and the infinite, the all-loving, the all-embracing, the all-powerful; here there are no clear limits. Here there is a need for commitment which continues to grow. The relationship is, in a very real sense, unique for each individual even though community involvement is retained. Here there is internal violence brought about by the constant struggle not to turn back and give up, not to lose hope, but to love yet more deeply.

How can we even begin such an arduous spiritual journey? The answer is the Holy Spirit, his gifts, his fruits, his presence, and above all, his love and gentleness. God allows us time to grow into our relationship with him. If we continue to show willingness, he will increase our understanding and our faith through the experience of prayers answered, disasters avoided (no thanks to us), and blessings unsought and unexpected. For those young in their faith, this might seem tenuous at first, but if we stay faithful, in time our relationship with him will rest on experienced realities. I consider this one of the best ways to understand baptism in the Holy Spirit. It is a benchmark in our spiritual growth, a point of maturity when we are able to produce more spiritual fruit than we consume. Our communication with God—i.e., our recognition of his voice—becomes strong enough that he can give us guidance and understanding in a direct and personal way, and we can respond in the way he desires, and thus the kingdom is built up. To say it another way, the spiritual gifts of 1 Corinthians 12 become a reality in our lives. Similarly, the fruits of the Spirit will be present.

Your Daily Life

This reflection on the Law is offered here for a couple of reasons. Primarily it is intended to help the reader deepen his understanding of the bigger picture, baptism in the Spirit and the process of spiritual growth. For the very young, the Law forms a set of initial restrictions on their lives; not only does this help them grow in obedience, but it also helps prevent a lot of damage they might otherwise encounter. With maturity, however, things change. The Law becomes a tool, like a GPS system, a quick reference on what is likely safe and what is not. Legalism diminishes (or at least it should), and the positive aspects of God's plan grow and replace it: personal relationship and mission, being part of God's family, direct awareness of your discipleship, and assurance of your great value to the Master.

A Disciple's Prayer

Come Holy Spirit, come.
Use me this day and always to serve Jesus as you would wish.
Come Holy Spirit, come.

Witness: First Bible Study

In the beginning was the Word, and the Word was with God, and the Word was God. He was in the beginning with God. All things came to be through him. and without him nothing came to be. What came to be through him was life. (John 1:1–3)

 We grow up learning the ways of the world. At some point there comes a change, one that is often quite abrupt—suddenly we realize that the kingdom of God is very different. Below Leonore Misner describes how that realization came to her. For me the situation was very different, but the change was just as abrupt and yet lasting.

Leonore: During parts of 1976 and 1977, we lived at Fort Leavenworth, where the Army assigned my husband to a full year of study at the Command and General Staff College. As a military wife, I was expected to "get involved" with worthwhile happenings and to socialize.

Even though this was a long time ago, I will never forget one thing that opened my mind and heart to a whole new life. We lived in a typical military housing area, where neighborhood gatherings were planned, such as a "coffee" that one of the ladies might host. I became friends with a girl who lived next door, Julie. She and I were both Catholic, and then we met Maria at one of the neighborhood coffees. Julie came over one day to tell me that Maria had invited us to the Post Chapel for a small Bible study. During my younger years, the Catholic Church did not condone reading the Bible on your own. That's right—we heard the biblical readings at Mass, and the priest would explain what those readings meant. So Julie and I both wondered if we should go to this Bible study. She had recently acquired a Bible and suggested that it couldn't hurt for us to become more familiar with it. I dusted off the one I had, and we went together to the study.

It was a small group, only five of us, but that encouraged intimacy. We began with the Book of John, which I have since learned is quite different from the three synoptic Gospels and does not follow the same order of stories as the others. On the contrary, it is a book of "signs" (miracles) that clearly affect the reader's psyche in a soul-searching way. The prologue "proclaims Jesus as the preexistent and incarnate Word of God who has revealed the Father to us.[10]" It declares the triumph of light over darkness; revealing Jesus as the light of the world. This Gospel truly characterizes Jesus as the Son of God, the Messiah, and teaches "that through this belief you may have life in his name." At the first study session, these words truly jumped off the page and hit me squarely between the eyes of my inner self.

Something else also caught my attention that day. The office girl of the Post Chapel poked her head into the room where we were discussing the Scripture passages, telling one of the ladies that she had received a phone call that her daughter had become ill at school. The mother called out "Praise the Lord!" as she put on her coat to get her little girl. Julie and I glanced at each other, thinking, *Well, that's weird—to sound happy after being told her daughter was sick.* Just as she was about to leave, the office girl returned, saying, "Oh, wait. The school called back and said the girl that was sick was not your daughter after all. The child had a similar name as yours." The mom exclaimed again, "Praise the Lord!" This time I sought answers from Maria, since this was her friend. Completely confused and dumbfounded, I wondered, *What did all this mean?* This woman thanked the Lord when she thought her child was sick, and again thanked him when she found out it wasn't her daughter who was sick.

As Maria read the Scripture verse, "All things came to be through him, and without him nothing came to be" (John 1:3), the revelation struck me that this mom wholly believed that if her

---

[10] From the introduction to the Gospel According to John of the New American Bible Revised Edition

daughter was sick, it was because God had allowed it. And if God allowed it, she could embrace it. Of course, when she found out that her daughter was not sick at all, she quickly praised the Lord again. I then saw this as a joyful declaration, and it reminded me of the fruit of the Spirit, especially joy. Oh, how amazing is God's work! One moment he writes on my heart the reality of the greatest truth: Jesus is the incarnate Word of God, the light of the world, and life comes through belief in him. Then the next moment he gently focused that same immense reality on my life in Fort Leavenworth where children become ill at school and wives struggle to support one another.

Galatians 5:22 lists the fruit of the Spirit as "love, joy, peace, patience, kindness, generosity, faithfulness, gentleness, and self-control." The wisdom of Christ and the experience of Christianity is that joy and the other fruits grow in our life when we set our hearts on God, on loving like he does, and on things of lasting value. When we cooperate with the graces and gifts of the Holy Spirit, we grow spiritually in all of these fruits. God gently prompts our awareness of how the Holy Spirit breathes new life into us. Simultaneously we should guard against being possessed by things of transient value—money, fame, power and influence, superficial beauty, and so on—but most important is keeping our focus on the positive values of the Christian life and seeking always to foster them for each person and in every situation. Gently but firmly, the light casts out the darkness. My first Bible study was certainly an unforgettable teaching moment!

Your Daily Life

The river of life is an ever-flowing, ever-changing process. Don't let the massive current disturb you; God has a plan for that. Instead, watch for the small things, the odd and unexpected item caught in an eddy. What is God showing you? Realize that each day gives you a new opportunity to see God's hand at work and to witness the passing touch of the Holy Spirit. Pause briefly to consider what might be revealed. It helps to begin your day with a phrase from Scripture,

105

and throughout the day take note of how that Scripture impacts your attitude and the decisions you make. Purposely observe your reaction to changes that occur throughout your day. Then, in the evening, replay the day's happenings in your mind. In what way did the Holy Spirit lead you?

A Disciple's Prayer

Spirit of Truth, I adore you and praise you. Breathe in me an awareness of your gifts throughout my day. Strengthen in me the resolve to put into action the fruit of joy during my day, no matter what happens.

Practical Spiritual Skills

In this section, we'll get down to
brass tacks on what a functioning
discipleship and our personal
relationship with God looks like.

Hear His Voice

The gatekeeper opens it for him, and the sheep hear his voice, as he calls his own sheep by name and leads them out. When he has driven out all his own, he walks ahead of them, and the sheep follow him, because they recognize his voice. But they will not follow a stranger; they will run away from him, because they do not recognize the voice of strangers." (John 10:3–5)

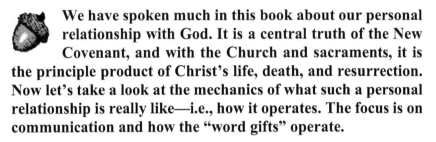 **We have spoken much in this book about our personal relationship with God. It is a central truth of the New Covenant, and with the Church and sacraments, it is the principle product of Christ's life, death, and resurrection. Now let's take a look at the mechanics of what such a personal relationship is really like—i.e., how it operates. The focus is on communication and how the "word gifts" operate.**

Our personal relationship with God is the source of the power and blessing of this renewal of Catholicism. In this relationship, two-way communication is essential; we must be able to hear and recognize God's voice. When we know we are hearing his voice, it is a strong indicator that the relationship is real and established, and that's a great boost to your faith. Of course, the real test is the fruit it bears; evidence of the fruit of the Spirit in our lives is the proof of the pudding. Keep in mind two important points: first, God is always working in our lives to the extent that we allow him, whether we recognize it or not. Baptism in the Holy Spirit means we recognize him and know it is God speaking. Second, the words *voice* and *hear* in this application must be construed broadly. We are all very different, and circumstances also differ greatly, so the actual communication may be verbal (prophetic), visual, or merely a subtle mental realization, and each of these has many variations. The following partial list should give you a sense of the breadth of possibilities:

- **Reading Scripture:** A verse jumps out at you, and you just know God is speaking that line directly to you then and there. This is often one of the first ways people experience communication with God after being baptized in the Spirit. Variations include looking for help with some question and opening and reading the Bible at some random location. Alternately, when you are quiet at prayer, God may make you aware of a particular psalm or section of Scripture. Less frequently, the same thing can happen when the words come from some other source, e.g., a comment from a friend or line from a book.

- **Prophecy (and visions)**: The forms of this can vary greatly. A message may come word for word or God may express to you the key ideas. At other times only the essence is communicated, perhaps by the flash of a vision or an understanding, and the person expresses the meaning in his or her own words. Frequently, perhaps always, some portion of the prophet's personality and vocabulary come through as part of the prophecy; thus, as with all forms of communication with God, discernment is needed to sort out what God is really saying and how his people should respond. Some prophecies give guidance, while others bring consolation, encouragement, or understanding. Indications of what to expect in the future are quite rare; the important point is generally the indication of how God's people should prepare. Also, concerning prophecies about the future, you will find your expectation of what will happen is most always off the mark, and the actual event will still be a surprise.

- **Dreams:** Scripture gives several good examples of communication in dreams, particularly in the accounts of Joseph in Egypt (see Genesis 40 and 41) and Joseph, Jesus' foster father (see Matthew 1 and 2). These examples are very prophetic, but in my own life some persistent dreams have been related to healing an inner sense of anxiety; they were always about an unfinished house and the great amount of worked needed to finish it. My father was a university professor by trade, but he built several houses for the family—some of the resulting anxiety must have rubbed off on me. I don't know how the healing worked, but it did.

- **Harmony:** This is also known as "pattern recognition." Sometimes you look at a sequence of events and just know that God is at work in that situation. There is a subtle combination of the rare or exceptional and the mundane, of everyday beauty or peace, that reveals that God's fingerprints are all over the situation. Today a friend called and told me a mutual friend had just discovered she had a serious medical condition. She had been estranged from her only daughter for two years, and all attempts to contact the daughter went unanswered. Our friend sent her daughter a simple text message: "I have [such and such] condition." The daughter replied immediately by phone. Is it worth getting a life threatening ailment to have a relationship restored? On God's scale, I suspect it might be.

As you can see, communication with God is a broad topic indeed. In a sense, it is describing what it is to live in God's household, and, of course, the answer is unique to each person. However, no matter how you experience God's communication, it never seems strange—rather, it fits very naturally with your human nature as well as your individual personality. There is nothing to fear from God.

Your Daily Life
Be steady, be faithful, and don't let yourself become discouraged. Remember, it is up to you to ask, to express your willingness to let God lead you, and to continue in your discipleship. Developing a close relationship with God is a lifelong process. You start where you are now, and you grow from there. Know that the relationship always exists; it is the improved communication you are waiting for. The maturing process takes time, even though baptism in the Spirit is often a single big jump. It might seem that day to day nothing changes, but if you keep a journal of what you pray for and what you struggle with, you will find that, when you look back

111

after a year or so, prayers have been answered, understanding has increased, and much growth has occurred.

A Disciple's Prayer

I call upon you; answer me, O God.
Turn your ear to me; hear my speech.
Show your wonderful mercy,
you who deliver with your right arm
those who seek refuge from their foes.
Keep me as the apple of your eye;
hide me in the shadow of your wings
from the wicked who despoil me. (Psalm 17:6–9)

Praise

Praise, you servants of the LORD, praise the name of the LORD. Blessed be the name of the LORD both now and forever. From the rising of the sun to its setting let the name of the LORD be praised. (Psalm 113:1–3)

A quick look at my concordance shows well over two hundred Scriptures that, like the one above, call on God's people to praise him. They are found from Genesis to Revelation, with the greatest concentration in the Psalms. The words and context vary, but the message is clear: God loves our robust, full-hearted, and full-throated praise.

"The dead do not praise the LORD." (Psalm 115:17)

"Give praise with blasts upon the horn, praise him with harp and lyre. Give praise with tambourines and dance, praise him with strings and pipes. Give praise with crashing cymbals, praise him with sounding cymbals. Let everything that has breath give praise to the LORD! Hallelujah!" (Psalm150:3–6)

Repetition in Scripture is usually a good indication of importance, so clearly praising God must have a very high priority. So, where has it gone? Robust cheers and praise are certainly not foreign to modern culture—just attend any sporting or entertainment event. But a religious event? Perhaps worldly culture has won a battle here that we are barely aware of.

I recall a prayer breakfast I attended in the early 1970s. It was my first experience of an event associated with the Charismatic Renewal. It was multidenominational but with quite a few Catholics present, and the speaker was a Catholic abbot. There were around two hundred people present, and before the talk began, they began singing, clapping, raising their hands, and praising God. I was standing off to the side, holding my arms straight down at my sides, wondering how to respond to what I was seeing. Something literally seemed to be gently but firmly pulling on both of my arms, trying to get me to raise them and join in the praise. I felt self-conscious and afraid of looking foolish. Later my foolishness became apparent to me; if 199 people are doing something together and one person is not joining in, it's pretty clear who looks foolish! Over time, as my wife and I became more and more involved with the Catholic Charismatic Renewal, I learned the correct name for my problem: "fear of man." I overcame it and learned to raise my hands and offer full-throated praise to God, much to my lasting benefit.

 With time it became clear to me why praise is such a primary feature of the Renewal; it is a door that opens us up to other, greater blessings. In prayer, praise helps focus our attention and put distractions aside. Then it draws us into a good attitude for prayer, recognizing that God is God, worthy of our praise and greatest respect. We are humans, most fortunate to be able to know and serve him. In our daily walk through life, when the crossfire of problems becomes intense, the habit of praise helps us keep our lifeline to God intact. It stirs up our faith and assures us that we can always trust in him. That's why the Scriptures tell us: "I will bless the LORD at all times; his praise shall be always in my mouth" (Psalm 34:2).

Your Daily Life

Through Confirmation, the Church calls us to be adult men and women of God, each standing on the firm foundation of God's love. Recall, they always emphasize courage in association with that sacrament. Beware of the fear of man! It will do its best to get you to fall short of where God calls you. We always should be open about our love for God. Whatever the situation you are in, no matter how long and difficult, no matter how hopeless, know that God is worthy of your trust and your praise. Choose praise, and you will find many blessings stemming from that choice.

A Disciple's Prayer

In as strong a voice as you can muster (but without waking the neighbors!), pray the three verses of Psalm 113 found at the beginning of this reflection. Do it over and over, and then let it draw you further into prayer. You will find a difference in the power of prayer when you pray out loud.

Watchfulness

Afterwards the other virgins came and said, 'Lord, Lord, open the door for us!' But he said in reply, 'Amen, I say to you, I do not know you.' Therefore, stay awake, for you know neither the day nor the hour. (Matthew 25:11–13)

For either teaching or just understanding Christianity, it's important to keep in mind the relative priority of the parables in Scripture; that is, the themes Jesus emphasized in his teaching and which therefore appear more frequently in the Gospels should draw our special attention. That is why we should focus on the master/servant relationship, Jesus' most common topic, and the kingdom of God, which is addressed almost as many times.

The topic of watchfulness is mentioned less often, but it still occurs several times in both the Old and New Testaments—most notably in Ezekiel 33, Proverbs 4:23, Matthew 24:42–50, Matthew 25:1–13, Mark 13:34–37, Luke 12:37–48, and 1 Thessalonians 5:1–4. In the Parable of the Ten Virgins, the ten virgins are awaiting the coming of the bridegroom. Five are wise and bring extra oil for their lamps; five are foolish and bring no oil. **Thus, the foolish 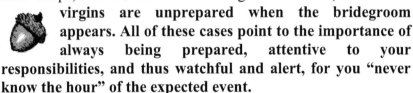 virgins are unprepared when the bridegroom appears. All of these cases point to the importance of always being prepared, attentive to your responsibilities, and thus watchful and alert, for you "never know the hour" of the expected event.**

The scriptural admonitions are clear enough; being watchful is primarily being attentive to God and to his will for a given situation. But a large part of that is simply remaining attentive to your responsibilities, without being prompted, without being monitored. Be attentive on your own initiative. The most important responsibilities come from your state in life: your family, job, state of health, and so on. Other responsibilities pop up as surprise situations—"out of the woodwork," so to speak. These situations might be due to a particular need, and sometimes they come from folks who don't want to take responsibility themselves and would rather try to pawn their own responsibilities off on others. These cases all require watchfulness. If the situation requires an immediate response, often the best you can do is a quick pause to listen and get a sense if God is speaking. Let God steer your perception — he will do that. Then ask yourself, "What would God have me do?" Thirty seconds seeking the Lord's guidance before you act can reap great benefits and prevent much grief.

A similar approach for quick, simple discernment, is to look at the question, "What does love require?" The answer can guide you to involvement, or stepping aside. Recall the Good Samaritan (Luke 10:29–37) and compare this passage with Luke 4:27, "Again, there were many lepers in Israel during the time of Elisha the prophet; yet not one of them was cleansed, but only Naaman the Syrian." God is always pleased that you make each particular situation a matter of discernment. Even when you get it wrong, he will find a way to bring a blessing

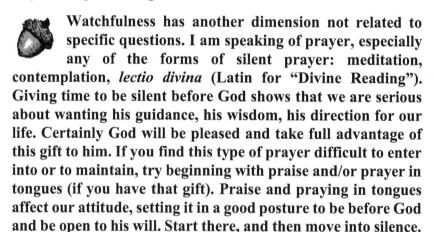 **Watchfulness has another dimension not related to specific questions. I am speaking of prayer, especially any of the forms of silent prayer: meditation, contemplation, *lectio divina* (Latin for "Divine Reading"). Giving time to be silent before God shows that we are serious about wanting his guidance, his wisdom, his direction for our life. Certainly God will be pleased and take full advantage of this gift to him. If you find this type of prayer difficult to enter into or to maintain, try beginning with praise and/or prayer in tongues (if you have that gift). Praise and praying in tongues affect our attitude, setting it in a good posture to be before God and be open to his will. Start there, and then move into silence.**

God can and will speak to us at any time, squeezing a word in edgewise into our busy minds. Once I went out to the street to pick up our recently emptied trash can. Spotting something shiny left in the bottom of the can, I reached in head and shoulders to retrieve the object. It was then that the Lord spoke to me about something that had been on my mind. . ... I was young in the spirit then, but the message was received. Of course, it is much better if we give him some peaceful quiet time each day so he doesn't have to fight for our attention. Watchfulness is a spiritual virtue, part of our spiritual growth process, so it's wise to make the effort.

Your Daily Life

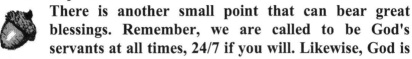 **There is another small point that can bear great blessings. Remember, we are called to be God's servants at all times, 24/7 if you will. Likewise, God is with us 24/7 to help, guide, and protect us. We should train ourselves to occasionally stop what we are doing and pause to discern, asking, "Is this what I should be doing?" A few seconds is all it takes. This especially applies when the task is long and/or we are getting tired, as these are the times when we are most likely to make a mistake, overlook something critical, or neglect something else we should be doing. Those few seconds reflection might save you a finger if you are working with power tools, provide you with a hot meal if your wife had it ready twenty minutes ago, or prevent a child's wrath if you are supposed to pick him or her up from soccer practice. Watchful servants also watch themselves.**

A Disciple's Prayer

Lectio divina is a traditional form of prayer with a strong relationship to watchfulness. Other forms of prayer typically emerge from your thoughts or emotions at the time, but *lectio divina* springs from a Scripture passage, often picked at random so it gives the Lord a chance to "change the subject." Pick up a Bible, open it, and start reading slowly. When you get to a verse and the Spirit nudges you (maybe you just don't quite understand what you've read), stop and meditate on the verse. Give it a few minutes of silent thought. What is God saying to you in those few words?

Lectio divina can be a real life saver during one of those sleepless nights when your emotions are worked up and your spirit disturbed by the events of the day. Perhaps praying a Rosary is in order for the specific issue, but then pick up the Bible and start reading slowly. Usually God will reset your perspective about the whole situation, and sleep will come much easier.

Tongues

[For] if I pray in a tongue, my spirit is at prayer but my mind is unproductive. So what is to be done? I will pray with the spirit, but I will also pray with the mind. I will sing praise with the spirit, but I will also sing praise with the mind. (1 Corinthians 14:14–15)

As we have been discussing in the preceding sections, being baptized in the Spirit is the door that opens everyone it touches to direct communication with God, and thus a very personal discipleship serving Jesus. It creates a zeal for building up the Church and a drive toward God's priorities such as personal integrity, unity in the body of Christ, and compassion for the poor. We can get a sense of just how powerful this move of the Spirit really is by looking at the gift of tongues, which is often considered as one of the lesser gifts. This should not diminish our regard for it, however, especially in terms of outreach. Even the smallest gifts of the Holy Spirit have immense, often life-changing value.

Let's begin with St. Paul's discussion of tongues in chapter 14 of 1 Corinthians. He spends a large segment of the chapter promoting the value of prophecy and other related gifts that unbelievers can understand and appreciate. The context for this discussion is the Christian assembly. He notes: "It is written in the law: 'Thus, tongues are a sign not for those who believe but for unbelievers, whereas prophecy is not for unbelievers but for those who believe'" (1 Corinthians 14:21–22). Paul's point is well taken. I have only seen it on rare occasions, but tongues can be off-putting to unbelievers and others who have not yet seen the blessings of the spiritual gifts. However, off-putting or not, it still is a witness that something new and powerful is happening there, especially since the prayer in tongues often draws the other spiritual gifts into play.

 The gift of tongues has value both symbolically and directly in the power of its use. The symbolic power

derives from the weakness Paul mentions. **Other than the choice to use tongues and how to use this gift—whether in a whisper or softly, or loud and boldly, or in song (this choice always rests with the person using the gift)—it is true that the mind is not involved. The Holy Spirit forms the words, so this is a simple yet profound example of surrendering ourselves to God. That surrender of self is the key to all Christian discipleship and the other charismatic gifts.** This is why some groups (but not the Catholic Charismatic Renewal) consider tongues as a necessary proof that baptism of the Spirit has occurred in a person. The Catholic Charismatic Renewal recognizes that other gifts can provide evidence of the baptism and, more importantly, it always keeps in mind that much spiritual growth and growth in the use of the gifts is yet to come after the initial baptism. Thus, speaking in tongues is a sign that reminds us of the path and beckons us into an ever-deeper relationship with our Lord. It may not use the mind, but it calls both mind and heart onward in the path of Christ.

Besides this symbolic power, the gift of tongues has its own direct powers. First, praying in tongues is closely related to praise; when tongues are interpreted, they are most often words of praise of God. As such, they have a powerful effect in drawing God's presence and power into a situation, whether it be during personal prayer in the quiet of the morning or in the gathering of a multitude of the brothers and sisters. This is one reason charismatic prayer meetings are so effective. Praise invites God's presence, while the attitude of surrender necessary for tongues puts people in good spiritual posture for prayer. What follows is often both powerful and profound. It might be prophecy, or it may be manifestations of the other gifts—spiritual, emotional, or physical healing or words of knowledge, and so on. Because it both draws God's presence and shows the fruit of our surrender of self, the gift of tongues is an important doorway to the other spiritual gifts.

The direct power of tongues appears most frequently in ministry situations, when someone with a problem has come to the community for prayer. No matter what the person says the problem is, there are often deeper issues the Lord wants to deal with in order to bring as complete a healing or resolution as possible. These may be issues that the person requesting prayer, let alone the prayer team, is not even aware of. Prayer is most effective when, like an arrow to its target or a hammer hitting a nail, it is right on the mark.

Sometimes the Spirit solves this by revealing a word of knowledge to someone on the prayer team. However, other times he uses tongues. For example, often in the middle of praying for a person, I will experience a shift in the language of my tongue. I might begin with my usual tongue (which probably would be interpreted as praise), but then there is be an abrupt shift to another voice of power (commanding but not harsh) in a different language. When more is needed than we have, God uses tongues to make up the deficit. These expressions of God's power still appear loving and gentle, but the results can be impressive. The Spirit is clearly at work even when we don't understand.

Your Daily Life

As St. Paul says, praying in tongues is a gift for the believer, and we believers need it to bring growth. We need it to be effective in what God would have us do. So if you have the gift of tongues, use it! If not, seek it! Seek baptism in the Holy Spirit if you have not yet experienced it. You will know it when you have it, so if there is question in your mind and it is more than three weeks since you asked for the baptism, pray and ask God to reveal and remove the obstacles. Pray with persistence for the gift of surrender to God's will. Always take an opportunity for someone to pray with you for more of the Spirit. God always gives the gift of the Holy Spirit to those who seek it, but he also gives increase in his gifts and manifests them when the time is right.

A Disciple's Prayer

If you have the gift of tongues, use it. If you don't, have someone pray with you to receive it. If you are not sure, try it anyway—

whether you are alone, or with your prayer group, or whenever the Lord brings it to mind. Remember, the Spirit forms the words, but you need to express them. It is our very human voice that must speak.

Real-Life Experiences

When something works, you may realize it was God's work. When you realize it was God, the whole idea of religion can change. One shortcoming of the typical parish is that there are few, if any, opportunities for sharing with the community experiences of God acting in our lives. Such sharing is very important because it does much to build not only our understanding of how God acts, but also our faith. Thus, the importance of informal prayer meetings and Bible studies becomes apparent.

Witness: Walking in God's Plan

The Spirit helps us in our weakness. We do not know what we ought to pray for, but the Spirit himself intercedes for us with groans that words cannot express, And, he who searches our hearts knows the mind of the Spirit, because the Spirit intercedes for the saints in accordance with God's will. (Romans 8: 26–27)

 Sometimes the harsh physical realities of this world drive us to the point where our heart falters. Even in this God has a plan. Here Leonore shares an example from her experience.

Leonore: Mom and Dad had lived in the Midwest their entire married life—for most of that time in the same house on a farm property. Happy as they were, the point had come when they could no longer sustain themselves out in the country, with grocery stores and drug stores being quite a distance from them. Dad, in his late eighties, should not have been driving, though he had to. My husband and I were living on the East Coast, and we located a suitable property in the Rhode Island countryside where they could live with us. We had to sell our home first in order to buy the other property, and Mom and Dad had to do the same. In the meantime, all we could hope for was that the property we wanted would not sell to someone else. We placed our fate in the Lord's hands, and we thanked the Holy Spirit for the peace he would give us.

The country home we wanted was one we knew my folks would really like. It was a forty-acre plot covered with deciduous and coniferous trees, with a cleared area where an eighteenth-century, two-story home sat. Attached to it was an "in-law apartment," perfect for Mom and Dad to live in—with a bit of enlarging. The most alluring feature was a three-acre pond within view of the house, where Dad could fish or just enjoy the peacefulness. This was truly God's country with a plethora of wild creatures; egrets visited there, along with geese and ducklings. Fish were there, too—at least until each year the freshwater otters slithered in by way of the small stream leading into the pond. They loved the pond, and they ate their fill of fish. The lush green grass in the surrounding area framed this animal sanctuary that Dad could enjoy for hours.

As faithful to God as Mom was, this move frightened her. Would the house sell? How would everything in the house get packed and reach the East Coast? What would life be like without the familiarity of where they had lived so much of their lives? Would it all work out? I reassured her that I knew God was with us, and we need not worry. I continually asked the Holy Spirit to guide us in this new venture.

We prayed for our homes to sell quickly. Both were on the market from March to July. In July things started to roll. Our homes sold within a week of each other! Mom and Dad's home in Indiana was built like a rock, literally. It was made of stucco with solid walls having a six-foot-thick base. But there was one issue: it was not up to code electrically. Thanks be to God, the buyer bought it with cash "as is," knowing he would have to do some electrical work. The Lord had planned it out seamlessly, because the folks who owned the plot in Rhode Island held on to the house for us until ours sold! "We know that all things work for good for those who love God, who are called according to his purpose" (Romans 8:28).

The process of getting Mom and Dad to their new home took a couple months. First, we rebuilt the "in-law apartment" to better accommodate their needs. Driving away from the hallowed halls of their home for the last time was very emotional, even for me. My growing-up years flashed through my mind as we looked back on the old homestead. My stomach ached at the thought that I would never again step foot in that home.

The Lord has a will, and we are meant to follow his will and rest in it. Having Mom and Dad with us the remaining days of their lives was a huge blessing. We have never regretted this turn in our lives.

Your Daily Life

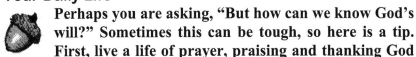 **Perhaps you are asking, "But how can we know God's will?" Sometimes this can be tough, so here is a tip. First, live a life of prayer, praising and thanking God for helping you get to this point in your life. Know that it is part of his larger plan. Second, humbly present your problem to the Lord. He already knows what it is, but it is in the presenting where he sees you "relinquishing" the problem to him. Simply voicing the dilemma in prayer will often prompt solutions. When you are in prayer the solutions that enter your mind, especially the "I never would have thought of that!" ones, are likely of God; start there and look for confirmation. Third, trust in the Lord, through the power of the Holy Spirit, to guide you through anything. Often you will find the answer only appears at the last minute**

A Disciple's Prayer

Holy Spirit, holy breath emanating from the Father to the Son, Our Lord Jesus, be with me, your humble servant, as I make this difficult decision: "Teach me, Lord, your way that I may walk in your truth, single-hearted and revering your name" (Psalm 86:11) in all I do.

Witness: Learning the Spiritual Ropes

Trust in the Lord and do good; dwell in the land and enjoy safe pasture. Delight yourself in the Lord and he will give you the desires of your heart. (Psalm 37:1)

Spiritual growth is a lifelong process, a long procession of small victories and occasional setbacks. Especially when you are new to the process and perhaps struggling, an example of how things work out in the long run can provide a valuable, encouraging perspective. Here is one such example from Leonore.

Leonore: I recently came across a piece from a 2009 Liturgical Publications, Inc., article called "How Do We Know When We Receive the Holy Spirit?" The author made a comparison between our earthly father and God the Father, prompting me to think about my relationship with my own father. My dad embodied a spirit of humility; he was a good man devoted to caring for his family. He was also a stern disciplinarian, a man who always believed in telling the truth and "doing what's right." At the same time, he had a gentle, quiet voice, when necessary expressing displeasure in a calm way.

When I was sixteen, Dad let me take the family car out for a drive. Since we lived in the country, we could walk to nothing but the neighbor's cornfield, and so driving became a necessity. Now, I was not the picture-perfect young lady, but my dad trusted me to do right by him. I picked up my girlfriend Karen, and we headed for the J.C. Penny's store in the mall. Karen coaxed me into buying a pack of Winston cigarettes. She and I slipped on high-heeled shoes that belonged to her big sister. Those shoes (not my size) cut into my feet and left me with stinging toes. We rode the elevator to the second floor, where she led me to the store's employee break room. We sat down with our legs crossed, trying to look sophisticated, and opened the pack of Winstons for a "smoke." In those early days of television, commercials portrayed iconic men and women smoking cigarettes as distinctively sexy. I had no idea how to do this smoking bit, and it quickly became pathetic when I tried to knock off the ashes by blowing at them in the ashtray. Before we left for home, I bought a pair of shoes that "fit," and the shoebox was a great spot to hide the cigarettes. When I pulled up to the house, my gentlemanly dad came out to help carry whatever I had bought. As he opened the back door, out fell the shoebox openly displaying the cigarettes. Scared and ashamed, I glanced at my dad, who simply said in a calm voice, "Oh . . . so now you're doing that." That's all he had to say. This sting hurt much worse than my toes. I never again put a cigarette up to my lips.

The main point of this poignant little reflection is my father's calm demeanor while expressing his disappointment in me. Disappointment? It was more than that—I had lost his trust. Love and authority are best expressed with a calm voice. It definitely made a lasting impression on me, and more importantly, it led me to enough introspection that other lessons came to light. An old proverb started to ring true: "Tell me who you go with, and I will tell you who you are." I certainly lacked perfection in choosing my friends. Where was that gift of wisdom they told us about in our Confirmation classes? Again, trying to look like someone I was not taught me that I was ignoring God's presence in my life. That day I had not made life choices with prudence; I had not lived as a faithful follower of Jesus. The light of the Spirit was not shining within me then, but it did shine on me in the form of my father's calm, measured expression of disappointment.

To tell you the truth, I didn't think very clearly back then. Yes, my Confirmation was at age fourteen, but despite what I had learned about this sacred sacrament, I spread my wings anyway (not angel wings either). As I look back at those formative years when my behavior was questionable, I now see how many times the Holy Spirit protected me in sordid situations. How does one make that transition from a newly baptized infant to a mature Christian who trusts in the Holy Spirit and whose earthly father can trust her? How does the Holy Spirit work during those formative years? We are born in the image and likeness of our Heavenly Father, albeit somewhat tarnished by "the fall" (i.e., the human condition). At Baptism we receive and at Confirmation we are sealed in the Holy Spirit. The Spirit himself is the most important "gift" of these sacraments; all other gifts flow from His presence; some soon, some much later. These gifts are like seeds that need to fall on fertile ground, grow and mature before bearing fruit (CCC 1153). However, although we may not be aware of the working of the Spirit, he remains with us, shielding our lives.

Speaking of gifts delayed, some clarification is required here. I am addressing the spiritual gifts that work through us, that involve our active participation. There are other gifts where the Spirit works *on* us—such as my father's calm expression when he saw the cigarettes and the way the Spirit alerted me that I had done wrong as I looked at my dad, instantly feeling scared and ashamed. The Lord is always trying to draw us to himself, often in such simple, natural ways.

In other words, the grace that flows from the sacrament depends on the response of the person receiving the sacrament—good soil is needed to produce good fruit. The gifts of the Holy Spirit depend critically on both our timely cooperation while using the gifts and our long-term growth in union with God.

Just as we grow from childhood into adulthood, we mature spiritually as we study the Word of God, receive the sacraments, and participate in the faith community. Our loving God gives us a free will to choose the right path, and on occasion we will miss the mark. The key is persistence, or faithfulness. Stay with the program and God will draw you into greater and greater harmony with the Holy Spirit. I have come to realize that we must trust in the Lord the same way the apostles had to trust the words of Jesus when he told them he would send the Holy Spirit to stay with them. In John 14:25–26 Jesus said:

133

"All this I have spoken while still with you. But the Counselor, the Holy Spirit, whom the Father will send in my name, will teach you all things and will remind you of everything I have said to you."

We can call on the Holy Spirit whenever we are confused or uncertain, in any situation where we want to know the truth. We can trust the Spirit to be our advocate, helping and comforting us during our life experiences. Reading the Book of Acts leads us to understand that the apostles, who were initially afraid for their lives after Jesus was crucified, later became "fired-up" with confidence after "all of them were filled with the Holy Spirit" (Acts 2:4). After that they completely trusted the Holy Spirit to strengthen them as they preached and taught about Jesus. That trust was not misplaced—God delivered them from many difficult situations.

Your Daily Life

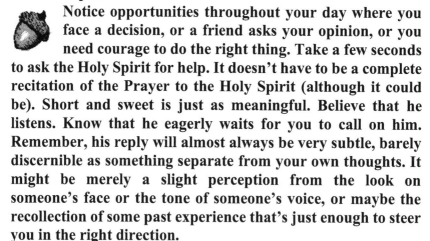 **Notice opportunities throughout your day where you face a decision, or a friend asks your opinion, or you need courage to do the right thing. Take a few seconds to ask the Holy Spirit for help. It doesn't have to be a complete recitation of the Prayer to the Holy Spirit (although it could be). Short and sweet is just as meaningful. Believe that he listens. Know that he eagerly waits for you to call on him. Remember, his reply will almost always be very subtle, barely discernible as something separate from your own thoughts. It might be merely a slight perception from the look on someone's face or the tone of someone's voice, or maybe the recollection of some past experience that's just enough to steer you in the right direction.**

A Disciple's Prayer

Praying to Jesus is like speaking to a friend. Use your own words, express your current thoughts, and keep it simple. "Jesus, help me" is often effective. Likewise, speak to the Holy Spirit the same way you would to God the Father or his Son, Jesus; speak the way you would to your own father or mother works. Whether in your regular daily prayer time or at the spur of the moment when faced with a decision, pray with an open heart and mind, asking the Holy Spirit to act in the situation and trusting that he will. Talking to the Holy Spirit can be as simple as "Holy Spirit, guide me in this." Eloquence is not needed—just sincerity and a dash of faith.

Witness: Trust in the Lord

Trust in the Lord with all your heart, on your own intelligence do not rely; in all your ways be mindful of him, and he will make straight your paths. (Proverbs 3:5–6)

 God neither slumbers nor sleeps, nor does he forget our earnest prayer. Here Leonore shares an example, though the path be twisted and the wait long.

Leonore: The four of us stood in a huddle in Ron and Donna's living room, arms draped over each other's shoulders, asking the Lord to guide us on the trek upon which we were about to embark. Only God knew the outcome, and we were trusting him.

They were old Army friends of ours, and Ron was one of those anomalies who always had a new idea, another invention taking him in a new direction. We called him the "wild inventor." But this time Ron really had something revolutionary, something that could work. He had come up with an antipollution device to install on diesel engines that would reduce the toxins discharged. He also had a cousin who was a lawyer and could help him set up a business. However, his cousin lived in Rhode Island, and we all lived in California. There was no getting around it; Ron and Donna would have to move. Ron asked my husband, Dale, to help him manage this undertaking. Dale and I prayed about this, and I knew we were meant to help Ron.

We had been grounded in California for several years after Dale retired from the Army. One position had recently ended, so Dale was open to something new, although this business proposition would uproot us once again after numerous moves during military service. As we prayed, I was convinced that God wanted us to take this enormous step in our lives. He wanted us to help Ron. But this would not be a military-assisted move; rather, it would be a move entirely on our own "penny." There were complications, not the least of which was a major earthquake in California that played serious havoc with Ron and Donna's home. By the time of the earthquake, Dale and Ron had relocated to Rhode Island, leaving Donna and I to sell our homes. Yet I was still absolutely sure we were making the right decisions, based on God's guidance. A year later, Dale and I purchased a home in Rhode Island, with Donna soon following. The start-up business was in full swing, backed by several investors.

At the same time my elderly parents were experiencing difficulties in Indiana. High winds with tornadic consequences caused several trees to fall on their home, leaving them with no electricity. Trees were down on all the country roads, so they were stranded. Friends helped them get through the devastation, but the event solidified their resolve to come live with us. Mom told me, "You know, Leonore, we won't leave Mickey behind." Since his "nervous breakdown" at age sixteen, my brother had been diagnosed with paranoid schizophrenia, and he lived at Mom and Dad's, with intermittent hospital stays. "Yes, Mom, I know," I told her.

There were more obstacles. The governmental emphasis on clearing air pollution was fraught with issues. Financial backing came to a halt, and eventually the company's board members bought out our shares. Their objective was to keep the plans and eliminate Ron and Dale altogether, which they did underhandedly. "Now what do you think of following God's will?" said Dale. He wasn't unbelieving, just questioning.

As I pondered God's direction in our lives, we were struck with another calamity. Consistent with his psychological past, my brother Mickey tried once again to take his life. Thank the Lord, we quickly got him to the hospital. The doctor told my parents that Mick could never live at home again, and she suggested a state hospital. This option was not acceptable to any of us. It was then that I discovered the real reason God sent us to Rhode Island.

We were able to place my brother in a group home, though this took some precious waiting time and effort. The manager of the home stressed that typically someone living in the group home had to die before there would be a place for a new person, but because the manager made special arrangements, Mickey got in. The manager told us, "Did you know RI has the most intensive system for the mentally ill? A great deal of emphasis is put on a place for them to live!"

I sat back, astounded. After all these years that Mom prayed for a safe place for her son to live out his life, the Lord answered. Here—in Rhode Island, the most unlikely state we would ever live—was the best place for my brother. This was the reason God guided us to this new life. This was why he brought us to Rhode Island. All along I thought we made this major decision for Ron's invention to take off. No, it was for Mickey.

As we stood in that huddle, the four of us, asking for God's providence, little did we know that he had bigger and better things for us. Ron quickly got a job with a great company, and he moved his family to Arizona. The move cost Dale and me our savings and some of my parent's savings, but that, too, was miraculous, because in the years since then we have recovered monetarily over and above what we lost. God is truly amazing, and he loves us beyond measure. Mickey still lives in Rhode Island, now in a fine nursing home. When we left for Colorado, we asked him if he wanted to move with us, and he said no. He is happy where he is. My mom is with the heavenly host, probably still praying for us all. Thanks, Mom.

Your Daily Life

 One final important point: if we make an honest effort to discern the proper path but somehow get it wrong, God will still be pleased that we made the proper effort. Whatever happens, be assured that he will be close at hand to help things turn out for the better.

A Disciple's Prayer

Lord Jesus, I wish to follow you faithfully as your disciple. Give me the gifts of discernment and courage that I might always recognize the path you have set for me and walk it in love.

Witness: A Fall in a Theater

But the one who gives us security with you in Christ, and who anointed us is God, he has also put his seal upon us and given the Spirit in our hearts as a first installment. (2 Corinthians 1:21–22)

Many are the afflictions of the righteous, but the Lord delivers him out of them all. (Psalm 34:19)

 God knows that spiritual consolation is often more important than physical consolation because it ministers deeper and lasts longer. The following is a great example from Leonore Misner.

Leonore: I have a debilitating disease that effects the stability of my muscles, so my excursions away from the comfort and safety of my home are measured and few. At the same time, I do enjoy occasional outings.

Recently, my daughter and a friend and I planned to see the movie *The Shack* and then go out for lunch. All three of us had read the book, and the movie proved to be just as inspiring. We never got to the luncheon, though, because of me. At the movie theater, my mistake was insisting to my daughter that I could walk to the bathroom by myself. As soon as I got out to the hallway, my walker went flying; I fell and briefly lost consciousness. I had banged my head hard on the thin, carpet-covered concrete. I felt nauseous, and no one was around to help. Despite it all, once I realized what happened, I struggled to get up. Returning to the movie, I opened those heavy doors to the theater, and it happened again. I flung forward, struck my head on the wall in front of me, and bounced to the floor, skinning my knees and jarring my neck, arms, legs, and head again. It was awful. Thankfully, my daughter heard me calling out for her. She helped me up, and shaken as I was, I returned to my seat to watch the movie.

The movie characterized a father who had lost his daughter to a heinous kidnapping and killing. This father eventually found security and wholeness in the personification of God in Three Persons at a shack. Understandably, the man had a hard time making peace with God because of his deeply wounded soul. Having lost his small child to such an evil onslaught by a malicious villain shattered any possibility of forgiveness. But as he opened his heart to the love of the Father, the grace of Jesus, and the gifts from the Holy Spirit, he began to soften.

When the movie was over, something miraculous happened. Emotions in the theater ran high, especially mine. I began crying uncontrollably. The movie theater cleared out. Then a black man walked up. Passing by my daughter, he came straight over to me and placed his hands around mine. He then began to pray. Deanna and Judy rested their hands on mine, too, while he prayed for probably five minutes. I bawled intensely.

I knew God had sent me an angel, just as he had for Deanna so many years ago when she had a car accident. She had been driving alone in the country in the evening, and as she came up over a rise, an old person was driving very slowly, causing Deanna to veer to the left quickly. Her car went into the median, and she was thrown to the floor on the passenger side, upside down. The Lord told her to reach over and push down on the brake pedal with her hand and then turn off the key. With great difficulty, she did so. Suddenly a black man appeared in the car and held her securely. When the police arrived, she asked about the man she wanted to thank. The police said, "There's no one here, ma'am."

In the movie theater, when this man came to pray over me, the Lord told me, "This is the same one that came to the aid of your daughter." The man hugged my head and left without fanfare. Deanna and Judy thought I knew him, but I did not, except for the thoughts the Lord put in my mind. God had given this grace-filled moment to me as a healing.

Your Daily Life

When we understand that nothing occurs apart from God, everything can be entered-into as a dimension of our journey with God. Even illness, war, poverty, and death are dimensions of the paradoxical sacredness of our less than perfect existence on this planet; for although they are not "intended" by God, they are part of the territory of human experience where God is to be discovered as a compassionate presence, one with us in our fear and pain. Life is no longer only sacred or secular, black or white—it is also a grace-filled gray.

A Disciple's Prayer

Lord, help me to recognize your wisdom in day-to-day happenings so that I might make the right choices. And grant me the gift of understanding so that I may see when someone is hurting or in need of compassion.

Witness: God and Computer Repair

Jesus said to his disciples: "Ask and it will be given to you; seek and you will find; knock and the door will be opened to you." (Matthew 7:7)

 God most often shows us his love and how near he really is in the smallest struggles of daily life. This reflection is a typical example, from Leonore's experience.

Leonore: It was one of those sleepless nights, so I got out of bed at 1:30 a.m. and headed for my computer. There is always something to do there: checking email, shopping, reading through my documents, or glancing at new sites. I enjoy sewing, so I could watch the latest video on sewing techniques. However, to my dismay, my keyboard wouldn't work. The keystrokes made a "ticking" sound on the computer; I could only get a few letters to show, then nothing. When things like this happen to me, I am relentless in determining the cause. So first I restarted my computer, but that changed nothing. Next I did a complete shutdown with a manual reboot. Still nothing. *Oh gosh,* I thought, *maybe this new keyboard I purchased has broken already.* With a sigh I disconnected it and reconnected the old keyboard. Same result—ticking and no key response. *Now what?* I'm not a computer techie, as you may have already guessed. I went through the usual routine pulling up the control panel, then hardware and sound. "That should do it!" I whispered. But alas, no. For me this was becoming a real challenge, and a maddening one at that. "Ah, Programs/Uninstall a program—let's check that out!" I found a recently installed program on drivers, one I did not authorize. I decided to uninstall it, after which the computer restarted. That was no help either.

At this point I was baffled. I could not get online to post a question. Frustrated, I talked to God, "OK, Lord, I can't sleep, I can't use my computer, and I don't dare start up my sewing machine for fear of waking my husband. My Bible is right here. Is that what you want me to do?" Then I bargained with him: "Please help me with this keyboard problem, and I promise I won't dedicate my time to the computer, but to you." As soon as I said that, an idea came straight to my mind. My husband's computer was right there. I could do a search on it! Hallelujah, I found a Q&A on exactly my keyboard issue. I followed those instructions, and lo and behold, it worked.

Sticking to my promise and thanking God, I pulled up the New American Bible site, in lieu of my own Bible, and I clicked on the phrase for "Today's Readings." The first reading was from the Book of Esther, when she was pleading with God for help. But the point still didn't hit me. In the Responsorial Psalm I read, "I will give thanks to you, O Lord, with all my heart" (Psalm 138:1–2). All right, that's good, yes—I thanked Him. Finally, the Gospel for the day hit me right between the eyes. Jesus said, "Ask and it will be given to you; knock and the door will be opened to you." Of course! I had asked, but that was not the first thing I did. I had waited until I exhausted all my options. Had I initially begun with an acknowledgment of God at my side, he would already have been working in me.

Your Daily Life

 Two things are at work here. First, you might be thinking, *This is a small thing. I'll save my prayers for something really challenging.* Now that's a bad idea; love is so often best expressed in the smallest of things, and love is what God is all about. Secondly, plan to set aside time to be with God. Every day carries its own challenges, big and small. God longs to reassure you, saying, "Let me help you through this day." How will you be with God today?

A Disciple's Prayer

Father God, I am a humble human being yearning for your guidance. Help me to find you in the simple things of life, so I will know you in the more complicated moments. May you breathe into me the gift of knowledge, that you may enlighten me about the obstacles of my day that keep me from you.

Witness: The Beauty of God Is Love

The voice of the LORD is over the waters;
the God of glory thunders,
the LORD, over the mighty waters. (Psalm 29:3)

God knows we need beauty; beauty is important. I learned that lesson one day on a scenic back-road in Alabama; there was, mixed together, mile after mile of natural beauty and the handiwork of hard-working people who cared about their environment. Here are some thoughts from Leonore, who experienced something similar in Yellowstone National Park.

Leonore: Have you ever been to Yellowstone National Park? There, the beauty of God's creation abounds. What God hath wrought is amazing, captivating even the most traveled individual! The forestry paints an incredibly beguiling banquet of colors and shapes that affect the viewer's emotional and spiritual balance. Truthfully, as you stand amidst this beauty, you might feel like you are at the gateway of heaven itself. Through the breath of God's Spirit, "The heavens declare the glory of God; the firmament proclaims the works of his hands. (Psalm 19:2)" Even before you know about the Holy Spirit, he has engulfed you.

We know from the Book of Genesis that God created the heavens and the earth and keeps them in existence. As Acts 17:28 says, "In him we live and move and have our being." We can see the beauty of his holiness in everything, but it's especially evident in the firmament of the earth at Yellowstone.

Framing the calm waters of Yellowstone Lake are towering lodgepole pines that cast a peaceful shadow over the landscape. Particularly interesting are the shapes of the lower boughs, and how at the very top, the trunk forms an arrow of bough-feathers pointing to its maker.

149

You become distinctly aware that this gorgeous site could only have been created by a loving God. There are no mistakes. There are no platitudes of monotony. There can be no judgment, because the One God in his infinitely perfect fashion has declared the beauty of his holiness.

This endless beauty flourishes in both minuscule and majestic ways. Microscopic algae live in the Grand Prismatic Spring. The complexion of the microorganisms ranges from a deep blue in the center to a radiating green and finally yellow with a tinge of orange at the edges. It's almost what we might imagine God's eye to look like.

His beauty in the majestic mountains is always overpowering. The magnitude of the landscape tells me that I am indeed small. Even with this realization, I am aware that my heavenly Father knows me and loves me. He has created such magnificence for his glory—and for us—and we praise his holy name.

God's almighty power is expressly demonstrable in the great waterfalls of Yellowstone, especially the mesmerizing Lower Falls. As the water leaps from astonishing heights, crashing on the rocks below, there may be a sense of fearful anticipation of its plight. However, in the book *Hinds' Feet on High Places*, author Hannah Hurnard writes, "Once over the edge, the waters are like winged things, alive with joy, so utterly abandoned to the ecstasy of the giving of themselves . . . as a host of angels floating down on rainbow wings, singing with rapture as they went." This poetic interpretation personalizes the waterfall in softer terms, as if Our Lord is anointing the passage of the water. Now the roaring thunder becomes a reservoir of happiness that continues to flow into the valleys below. Like these life-giving waters, God purifies our souls through the sanctifying grace of the Holy Spirit. And sanctifying grace makes us holy and pleasing to God.

The Holy Spirit dwells in the Church as the source of its life and sanctifies souls through the gift of grace. The Bible tells us, "Take as your norm the sound words that you heard from me, in the faith and love that are in Christ Jesus. Guard this rich trust with the help of the holy Spirit that dwells within us" (2 Timothy 1:13–14). The beauty of God is expressed in a multitude of ways, laying for us a solid foundation of love on which to build an edifice of our faith.

Your Daily Life

There are many fruits of the Spirit beside those listed in **Galatians 5:22, and one that certainly should be added is appreciation—appreciation of God, of who he is, of what he has created, and of what he has given us. He knows we need beauty, and he has provided it. We need the soothing sounds of waterfalls and surf and wind, and he has provided those in abundance. He knows that we need friends and competition and flowers and things to surprise us and cause wonder; all this he has provided in abundance. At least once each day, try to pause and express appreciation for these blessings, not only for what your see or feel, but also for the God who resides within your heart. Remember that he is enjoying the moment with you.**

A Disciple's Prayer

Praying the Psalms has always been a great blessing to me. Over and over during my morning prayer time, a number would softly appear in the back of my mind. Was that my mind or the suggestion of the Holy Spirit? Either way, I would read and pray the psalm with that number and, many more times than not, it would give me just the word I needed to hear. Today, read Psalm 29 slowly as a prayer. What thought did it stir in your mind? Recognize that true happiness comes from knowing and following Christ, who gives you new life.

Personal Practices: Renewing the Church

Better discipleship, where each individual is led and empowered by the Holy Spirit, is the key to God's renewal of the Church, a renewal that is reaching deep into American culture. It includes better discernment of God's will, brighter shining forth of the light of Christ, person-to-person moves toward increased Christian unity, and healing the ills of the Christ-less world.

154

Guidance and Discernment—The Keys to Discipleship

Set up road signs; put up guideposts. Take note of the highway, the road that you take. (Jeremiah 31:21, NIV)

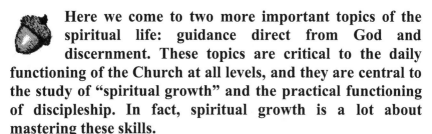 **Here we come to two more important topics of the spiritual life: guidance direct from God and discernment. These topics are critical to the daily functioning of the Church at all levels, and they are central to the study of "spiritual growth" and the practical functioning of discipleship. In fact, spiritual growth is a lot about mastering these skills.**

Here we are only able to provide a foundation of some of the wisdom that has come from the Renewal, but it will give a good sense of where to begin and the confidence that there are, indeed, good answers.[11] An important note before we get into the details; it has long been part of the Christian tradition for people facing significant issues in life to discuss them with their pastor, parent, or spiritual advisor—someone they love and respect. This applies equally to both the young as well as the spiritually mature; in fact, its value increases as one's Christianity matures because the decisions one must make often become more difficult.

So how do you, as a faithful servant, carry out this responsibility to be Jesus' disciple on a day-to-day basis? Of course, the first answer is *don't sin* and observe the Ten Commandments, the Beatitudes, and other teachings of Christ and the Church. This is always an initial condition. However, for good discipleship, this is not enough. Think of the problem this way: imagine that you are visiting Bryce Canyon or one of our other national parks with a scenic vista. The park service has placed guard rails and warning signs all around in order to keep you from falling to quick and utter

---

[11] You will find a more extensive discussion in the latter chapters of B. Jeffrey Anderson's *The Narrow Road: A Catholic's Path to Spiritual Growth* (Create Space, 2014).

destruction. The commandments and some Gospel teachings are like that guard rail; they keep us out of trouble, but they are not detailed enough (nor are they intended) to lead us in effective discipleship. More is needed: effective discipleship is like dancing with the Holy Spirit; he leads and we follow, responsive to his subtle, guiding touch.

Guidance and discernment are separate topics, but they are so linked and intertwined in the life of a Christian, in following Jesus as a disciple, that it is best to discuss them together. Guidance refers to communication, seeking and receiving the ideas which are communicated by God (or perhaps not). Discernment, on the other hand, refers to the decisions which follow: *Was that idea from God? How should I respond?* Thus, discernment is a matter of reason; guidance is a matter of perception. Notice that here we are limiting the discussion to determining a course of action that God wishes us to take. The term *discernment* may also be applied to seeking understanding of oneself and/or the internal or external spiritual struggles with which one must deal; that is a separate, though related, subject.

First, to explain the basic ideas, let's look at a simple case such as "What do you want for dinner?" Then we'll consider how the process evolves for a serious, life-changing question such as "Should I marry him/her?" The elements of guidance and discernment are multiple and overlap in the different cases, while the principles are the same for both. For serious questions, a lot more prayer, time, and work is needed and some additional tools come into play. We'll take the simple case first:

My wife asks, "What do you want for dinner?" Worldly culture leads me to take the question at face value: What hits the desire of my palate? Why, steak smothered in onions, a baked potato, and Brussel sprouts. How easy it is to let that quick, short-term desire drive my answer! But usually other factors enter in, and from a Christian worldview, the criteria are quite different: How is my wife doing? Does she really want to cook or does she need a rest? Do I need to keep the preparation simple? Who else will be eating with us? What foods do they dislike or are unable to eat? Is cost an issue? Must someone make an extra trip to the store? The list could go on, but the point is simple; even a question such as what's for dinner can easily impact a lot of folks. When we consider the needs and desires of others, we show our love for them, and they feel loved. Wearing my Christian hat, can I still consider my own desires? Yes, to some extent, but Christian culture leads us to keep the larger picture—the needs and wants of others—in the forefront.

From the charismatic perspective, another factor needs to enter the decision-making process: the voice of the Holy Spirit. The Spirit may speak when we are faced with a decision, especially when we pause and ask, or at any time when he wants to redirect our planned course of action. Sometimes the consequences are life-saving, as we've seen. But the need to be sensitive to the Spirit's guidance also applies to the simplest, routine decisions of daily life.

One day, early in my career at NASA, I was walking down the long halls of our building headed for my office when I sensed the Spirit say, "You need to get started." The reference was clearly to the preparation of an experiment pallet we needed to assemble and prepare for flight in about six months. That seemed like plenty of time for the task, but it wasn't. Fortunately, I paid attention to the prompting and we were ready on time, but it was close. Another day on the same project, I had three quick tasks to perform, and I headed off to do them in order—A, B, C. The Spirit clearly warned me to change the sequence, but I ignored him, and what should have taken ninety minutes to accomplish ended up taking all afternoon. At every stop it seemed I had just missed the person I needed to see.

To summarize, the discernment process goes something like this:

> Step 1: Look around and think. Where are the guard rails? Are you dealing with discipleship or temptation? A key point: God's guidance most frequently comes by perception—i.e., what he calls to our attention. This works

157

for everybody; but baptism in the Spirit makes it easier to identify God as the source.

Step 2: Pause and "test the Spirit"—that is, ask for guidance. Mostly this is just quieting your brain so God can insert a word or idea. If the Spirit gives you a sense that a certain answer is best, then follow that path. At this point you might find an obstacle popping up, such as fear of looking foolish or being rejected. Press on—fear is not of the Lord. Know that in many cases the Spirit will not answer; nothing will come to mind. This means that either the answer doesn't matter with respect to God's plan, or he knows the best answer matches your desire. In those cases there is one more check to make (see Step 3), but basically you are free to choose what you want.

Step 3: Does your answer mean something to anybody else? If the answer is no, you are free to choose what you want. If others are involved, choose what seems best and meets the wishes of all concerned.

The primary principle involved in this sequence is that God's plan is always better and thus always takes priority. Our plans and desires come into play when there is no conflict with God's direction. I would submit that this is the meaning of "deny yourself" in the normal, day-to-day definition of discipleship. Notice also how guidance (looking for God's input) and discernment (the exercise of reason) alternate and work together to help us make a good decision. It does not take a lot of time or effort on our part, but it does require an awareness of the situation (watchfulness) and reasoning based on sound principles.

When the question at hand is a serious, potentially life-changing matter, these principles and basic process still apply, but much more time and care should be taken to discern the answer. In addition, some additional principles can come into play:

The best test of a course taken is the fruit it bears. If a decision brings love, joy, or peace, especially in the long term, it was most certainly a good one. Similarly, in interactions with other people, the fruit from decisions and experience early in a relationship will often help in discernment of later, more serious commitments (for example, dating before marriage). Fortunately, for the majority of life-changing decisions, one is able to "sample" the answer and look for the fruit it bears. The fruit that results is always one of the best indicators of the correctness of a decision (see Matthew 7:17, among many other Scriptures).

Are your actions loving? God not only always acts in love, he is love. Love is his essential nature. So, if you are to grow spiritually and be true in your life-choices, you must grow in self-giving love.

Charismatic promptings need to be tested. Here clear communication with God enabled by prophecy, visions, or other gifts of the Spirit is obviously important. For small matters, discernment of the Spirit's promptings can and should be very quick: you pause, consider the other guideposts, and ask yourself if you are comfortable that it was from God. Yes? Then respond. You will learn to recognize the Lord's voice. Just like the voice of a friend on the phone, on occasion you might wrongly identify it, but ninety-nine times out of one hundred, you get it right. For more weighty matters, when consequences are more likely to be lasting or significant, much more caution is called for. Look for confirmation of the prompting and consider the reliability of the source. Are your emotions likely to be influencing your decision? What is the cost of delay to await more fruit or confirmations to appear?

Fulfill your responsibilities. Pay close attention to fulfilling the responsibilities of your position in life. God has placed us in positions we are competent to handle without micromanagement, and he leaves it like that. In reality, God has been training us to think "like him" over the years of our

159

discipleship, so we know how we should act. Therefore, do not expect active guidance for each question you face; God expects you to use your brain and your understanding of his ways. Like the Scripture passage at the beginning of the chapter says, "Take note of the highway, the road that you take."

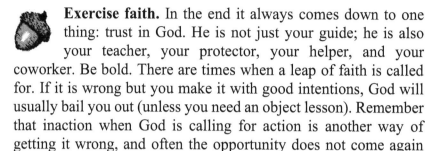

Exercise faith. In the end it always comes down to one thing: trust in God. He is not just your guide; he is also your teacher, your protector, your helper, and your coworker. Be bold. There are times when a leap of faith is called for. If it is wrong but you make it with good intentions, God will usually bail you out (unless you need an object lesson). Remember that inaction when God is calling for action is another way of getting it wrong, and often the opportunity does not come again anytime soon.

Guidance and discernment are, or at least should be, normal facets of life for all Christians—in fact, for all people. This is how we are intended to operate. **The most important point here is that we look for God's guidance with the intent of following it. Here Scripture and Church experience and teaching represent vast and critical resources to give us support.**

Your Daily Life

It is worth saying one more time: your actions should be compatible with Church teaching, especially Scripture and the Ten Commandments. Centuries of experience have shown this, invariably, to be the smart thing to do, even when it comes with a significant price to pay in the short run.

As you spiritually mature—and especially after baptism in the Spirit— you will rapidly become more familiar with the spiritual gifts and also experience a more active, charismatic dimension of God's guidance. Active guidance is needed to make us effective in ministering to others and thus building up the Church. It prompts us to take a specific action—whether a lifestyle change, an act of ministry, or some other action that expresses God's love. Most of the spiritual gifts we have already covered in this book are actually practical helps in this regard.

Don't fret when God is silent—remember, he does not micromanage. He only intervenes with guidance when it matters, when a blessing to you or someone else is at stake. God made us all talented, intelligent human beings in his image. As we follow the Christian walk, we become more and more like him. Thus, often specific guidance is not needed; we know what God wants us to do. If we stumble across someone in trouble, we know we should help as best we can. Practice is needed, and good practice is simply to pause, still your mind, and listen for the Spirit before making small decisions. If the Spirit is silent, it is up to you—your choice.

A Disciple's Prayer

To you I raise my eyes, to you enthroned in heaven.
Yes, like the eyes of servants
 on the hand of their masters,
Like the eyes of a maid
 on the hand of her mistress,
So our eyes are on the Lord our God,
 till we are shown favor. (Psalm 123:1-2)

We Need Community

There is no question that modern American society is very mobile, especially in comparison to pre-World War II America and the "old country" our ancestors came from. In fact, census bureau statistics indicate that the average American moves every five years. Between 2012 and 2013, over 11 percent of the population moved.[12] Mobility of that magnitude is an obstacle to the development of close, vibrant community groups, and the problem is aggravated by the ultra-busy American lifestyle with both husband and wife working and the kids immersed in school, sports, and extra-curricular activities. Parish structure and tradition were developed during the less-mobile age, so changes are needed, and are indeed occurring, to help foster effective small communities.

 So why are small communities needed? First, and perhaps foremost, they provide the human connection that all of us need. They provide a place where each person's voice can be heard, so that the sense of belonging and of value to the community becomes realized. This is particularly critical for those of us who are not yet aware of a personal connection with the Lord, but the need is there for everyone. Of course, regular participation in the larger (parish) community and sacraments are essential, but these alone can leave an individual feeling isolated and unloved.

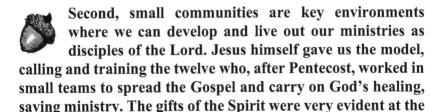 **Second, small communities are key environments where we can develop and live out our ministries as disciples of the Lord. Jesus himself gave us the model, calling and training the twelve who, after Pentecost, worked in small teams to spread the Gospel and carry on God's healing, saving ministry. The gifts of the Spirit were very evident at the**

---

[12]Joshua Green, "How Often Do Americans Move, and Why?" November 18, 2019, *Moving Guides.* Read more at:
https://www.mymovingreviews.com/move/how-often-and-why-americans-move/.

beginning of the Church, and they continued down through the centuries in the work of the saints. **In our current day, since the outpouring of grace through the Charismatic Renewal, the effects of the gifts have been explosive in many parts of the world, but they most frequently operate in very small groups, with a few people ministering to one another.** Besides prayer groups and other expressions of the Charismatic Renewal, effective teams include all groups where the presence of the Holy Spirit is manifest, groups that minister to the poor, music groups, sacristans and other parish support teams, ministry to prisoners, the elderly or infirmed, teaching, and charitable organizations. Both the gifts and the needs are many and diverse. Keep in mind that it is all the work of the Holy Spirit, and we are just the (very necessary) servants that he uses to make it happen. The Jesuits have a saying that can help us keep the right perspective: Work like everything depends on you; pray like everything depends on God.

Your Daily Life

Even when you have a mature and direct relationship with the Lord, you are likely to encounter seasons when he seems remote, when confusion seems to dominate, or when you badly need a fixed point to help you keep your bearings. Community is a major aid in overcoming these rough spots; let me explain. Over the years God, in a prophetic sense, has given me several pictures which have served me as fixed points when I needed them. Let me share one such picture that relates to community. It came to me in a flash vision while I was on retreat at the Ark and the Dove in Pittsburgh, the birthplace of the Charismatic Renewal some fifty years before.

The vision was of a broad landscape, hills and forests and open areas. The night was very dark; I could barely make out the scene. I sensed two other things: first, I was with a small squad of soldiers, and we were breaking camp and getting ready to move out into the night. Second, though they could not be seen, that entire landscape was filled with thousands of such squads like ours, each alone and independent of the others, but each moving out on their mission.

164

God was making his move. The point of the vision seemed to be that first, God has it all in hand, and second, a call for prayer for the captains, the squad leaders. The success of each mission rested on their shoulders.

I believe this vision has yet another point that also applies to each of us: Find your squad! While each call is unique to each individual, it is almost never a solitary call. It will be a call to a team that, like a squad of soldiers, works together, supports each other, and watches each other's back. Each soldier has a specialty, a unique role, and each is needed for the mission. Your initial squad may be primarily for training, to provide an environment where you can grow in the spiritual gifts, in wisdom, and in the skills and faith you need later to accomplish more critical missions. Remember, the servant who proves faithful in little things is given greater responsibilities. Learn the lessons well, because it may not be long before you find yourself gathering others around you to form a new team.

A Disciple's Prayer
Lord, lead me to my squad! My desire is to be a part of a team that will help me to grow in the spiritual gifts so together we can accomplish kingdom missions.

Be a Light—Shine Your Light

You are the light of the world. A city set on a mountain cannot be hidden. Nor do they light a lamp and then put it under a bushel basket; it is set on a lampstand, where it gives light to all in the house. Just so, your light must shine before others, that they may see your good deeds and glorify your heavenly Father. (Matthew 5:14–16)

In times past it may have been easy to gloss over this passage without too much notice. We might have taken it as a compliment—our good deeds will make us "shine" in the world. But in recent decades the pressure of secular society to keep our religious beliefs secret—hidden so they cannot impact other people in any way—has grown to the point that it has become a primary political force. Sure, we are still free to worship as we choose in our private gatherings, but pray in school or before a football game? Pray at the office when a coworker has fallen ill? Certainly not. Instead, we are told to pause for a moment of silence—I guess so we can fret on how bad the situation is! Christmas party—no, make it holiday party. Around every corner it seems we encounter a focused attack on actions that express our religious beliefs. There is also a real effort to force us to participate against our will—to officiate or sell cakes for same-sex "weddings" or provide pills or medical insurance that cover birth control and abortions. **Rather than just another Scripture passage, the matter of letting the light of Christ shine out brightly, being a lamp set high where it cannot be missed, is now at the center of the battle between Christianity and secular culture.**

So how do we fight this battle—and how do we win it? First, we must remember that a lamp is an instrument that illuminates; it shines to show beauty and truth. It is not very useful as a club with which to beat someone over the head, and in such cases the lamp itself is usually destroyed. Just as a moth is drawn to the light, we

167

humans also stop to admire the beauty of city lights. The illumination Jesus is talking about comes from who we are, the things we do, and the things we say. The good shepherd "walks ahead of them, and the sheep follow him, because they recognize his voice" (John 10:4). That voice is still here, still available to us. It is the voice of Jesus transmitted by the Holy Spirit to us and through us. It is the voice others hear when we speak of hope, faith, or love. They hear when we speak softly the simple truth, or words of encouragement, peace, joy, and beauty.

The voice of Jesus is also present when we speak of forgiveness, of peace and not anger. Recently there have been a number of exceedingly strong witnesses to the power of Christ—cases where senseless brutality or killings have been followed by words of forgiveness and peace spoken by the victims or their relatives. These cases illustrate the sublime truth that Christ won for us on the cross: victory over sin not by fighting against it but by absorption. Jesus drew the evil into himself, removing its effects from the world and providing a path of healing and salvation to all who follow him. Even before the Cross, the world heaped plenty of scorn upon Jesus. As his followers, we can expect the same treatment, so we need the Holy Spirit's gift of courage. Courage then becomes something we give others by our example.

Jesus did what he did out of love for us because he knew it was worth it. Is it worth the cost for us also? You bet! Just look at the bigger picture. First, Jesus has already "overcome the world"—his victory is already assured. Second, for a lamp to shine forth in hope, faith, love, beauty, truth, peace, and joy, it must be filled with those very same things. What better way is there to live? Finally, there is the matter of time. Evil is transient and passing away; evil tends to destroy itself. Hope, faith, and love, on the other hand, endure forever. "Love never fails" (1 Corinthians 13:8). The blessings of the Holy Spirit remain now and forever.

How has the charismatic dimension of Christianity altered this picture? If you understand that the gifts of the Spirit (1 Corinthians 12, Ephesians 4 and Romans 12) are each manifestations of God's love, the answer is pretty evident. The gifts "build up the Church" by building up one, or perhaps a small handful of people at a time. By providing direct experience of God's power to console, guide, heal, restore, and encourage, the gifts witness God's love directly to the person benefiting from the gift. Even when the gift is delayed, as when a healing takes some time to manifest itself, the fact that somebody took the time and had the courage, faith, and concern to stop and pray to manifest the gift is an extremely powerful expression of love.

However, as powerful as this is, there is yet another deeper and more powerful stroke. A primary obstacle Christians face to letting their light shine for Christ is "fear of man." This can be a fear of rejection, a fear you won't do well, or some other fear, usually ill-defined and not really rational, that freezes us in place and prevents us from witnessing. Fortunately, baptism in the Spirit and the fellowship of Charismatic prayer meetings are very effective in enabling the Spirit to increase our zeal and grow our faith so that this and other obstacles can be overcome. **One quickly finds that when evangelistic efforts are perceived as expressions of love, and not intellectual exercises or arguments, they are almost always well received. Again, the gifts of the Holy Spirit are all about expressing God's love. When a person really perceives that God loves them, the rest of the evangelization process falls into place pretty easily.**

Your Daily Life

You are invited to enter the reign of God—the reign of love, beauty, truth—and to shine with that light. Your call begins in earnest with your Baptism and your entry into God's household. It grows as you do. With the sacraments, that call grows ever more serious and the spiritual tools available to you increase. You are meant to bring hope, faith, love, and the other fruits of the Holy Spirit to those around you. It is a matter both of who you are and what you do. Curiously, this is all in your best interest; joy and love are what we all want to experience. Meanwhile, selfish desire and fear are the greatest obstacles to your success. Pray constantly for the Holy Spirit's presence and courage, and by prayer, keep your eyes on the true goal.

A Disciple's Prayer

LORD, who may abide in your tent? Who may dwell on your holy mountain?

Whoever walks without blame, doing what is right, speaking truth from the heart; Who does not slander with his tongue, does no harm to a friend, never defames a neighbor; Who disdains the wicked, but honors those who fear the LORD; Who keeps an oath despite the cost, lends no money at interest, accepts no bribe against the innocent.

Whoever acts like this shall never be shaken. (Psalm 15)

Witness (Part A): A Precious Vessel

In a large household there are vessels not only of gold and silver but also of wood and clay, some for lofty and others for humble use. If anyone cleanses himself of these things, he will be a vessel for lofty use, dedicated, beneficial to the master of the house, ready for every good work. So turn from youthful desires and pursue righteousness, faith, love, and peace, along with those who call on the Lord with purity of heart. (2 Timothy 2:20–22)

In the many years I have been following the Lord, I have found few, if any, Scripture passages that have meant as much to me as this one. Let me explain why. One evening in 1977, we hosted a dinner party for twenty or thirty folks from our Christian community; the occasion was a visit by a leader of a similar community from out of state. At the end of the evening, as our guest was saying his goodbyes, I overheard him say to someone, "I will be there if I have to crawl; I think something really important will happen there." He was referring to an upcoming international Charismatic Renewal conference to be held in Kansas City. I knew of the conference and had not given it much thought, but those words stuck in my brain. I was traveling for business the week before the weekend of the conference, and at the last minute I changed my flights and flew to Kansas City Friday evening.

The first lesson the Lord had prepared for me began at the rental car desk. When I said I did not have a reservation, the agent said, "Oh, we may be sold out." As it turned out, they had one car left. On finding out I did not know where I was going to stay, he said, "There must be something big happening in town—people are driving to Lawrence [roughly thirty miles away] to find a room." Driving into town, I recalled something my father once told me: you can always find a motel room by leaving the freeway and taking the old highway into town. I quickly found a vacancy in an

171

old hotel very near the conference center; a very nice room, probably the largest I have ever stayed in and at an extremely reasonable price. The last part of this lesson came the next day over lunch at a fast-food place next to the conference. Alone for lunch, which I always hate, I struck up a conversation with a man, his wife, and one of their mothers. They were also attending the conference and, being new to the Renewal, they were full of questions, which fortunately I was able to answer. More than that, it seemed we were kindred spirits. We just hit it off, and they proved excellent company for the rest of the weekend. **To me the lesson was clear: God had wanted me at that conference, and he had prepared everything for me, everything I could possibly need or want. Out of all his people, all his servants, he had selected me and put me there. I doubt I could ever receive a greater honor.**

The next lesson came from one of the keynote speakers, Sr. Ann Shields. She used the above passage from 2 Timothy during her talk Saturday morning. **The Spirit's message was clear and stamped in my heart: if I wanted it badly enough, if I made it my priority and worked at it, I too could be a useful, noble vessel in the Lord's house.** Most of us have several little objects we continually use and keep near us—a mug with a pleasing design, an easy chair, a favorite hat, or well-used tool. (My list includes a hammer that was a gift from my mother-in-law and a forty-year-old scientific calculator that works in Reverse Polish notation.) We keep these things close and repeatedly choose them first because they fit our need, our hand, our spirit—they fit who we are. Paul's letter to Timothy tells us it can be that way with God. I can see myself now: God's mind is who knows where—the Middle East, Washington, D.C., the plight of some lost child in Florida? Who knows? But I know where I am—I'm that mug a quarter-full of almost-cold coffee, still warmed by God's hand that continues to hold me while his mind is far away. What a gift!

For the record, our visitor was right about the importance of the conference. My life was not the only one which was profoundly touched. Continue to "Witness (Part B): Christian Unity" for the rest of the story.

Your Daily Life

You may or may not realize it at the time but going out of your way to grow closer to God always brings a blessing. Whether the event is a conference, a teaching, a Mass, or a lowly prayer meeting with two or three people, it matters not; God takes note and blesses you for your faithfulness and effort. Of course, the proper attitude and preparation, your "response of faith," will add to that blessing (see *CCC*,1153) We know God's love for each of us manifests in many ways, but knowing and feeling it most tangibly often comes in response to our effort and service to him.

A Disciple's Prayer

Dear Lord, I am your servant. Help me to serve you well today.

Witness (Part B): Christian Unity

"I pray not only for them, but also for those who will believe in me through their word, so that they may all be one, as you, Father, are in me and I in you, that they also may be in us, that the world may believe that you sent me. (John 17:20–21)

The preceding reflection recalls how I got to the conference in Kansas City and how the Lord personally touched and guided me. **There was, however, something much more important that I witnessed, something that should touch us all. It reveals God's feeling and passion for Christian unity. Substantial progress has been made in this regard since 1977, and the role of the Charismatic Renewal clearly has been important, particularly because the charismatic gifts give us a great common experience with many non-Catholic communities. If, however, you have any doubts about the path ahead or question God's priority, please continue reading.**

Notes from Kansas City 1977 Conference on Charismatic Renewal in the Christian Churches

Two prophecies were given at the Saturday evening session of the conference, and I felt the words to my core. Like a one-two punch, the second prophecy followed immediately after the first.[13] The experience holds a strong influence on my attitude toward inter-church relationships to this day. My recollection of the confirmation of the second prophecy is given at the end of that prophecy.

First Prophecy

I believe that the Lord has a word to speak to the leaders of all the Christian churches. If you are a bishop or a

---

[13] Both prophecies were published in *New Wine* magazine, October 1977, p13. One was presented by Bruce Yocum, the other by Ralph Martin.

superintendent, or a supervisor, or an overseer, or head of a Christian movement or organization, and that includes many of us here, this word is for you.

Because the Lord says you are all guilty for the condition of My people, who are weak and divided and unprepared. I have set you in office over them and you have not fulfilled that office as I would have had it fulfilled, because you have not been the servants that I have called you to be. This is a hard word but I want you to hear it.

You have not come to me and made important in your lives and in your efforts those things which were most important to Me. But instead you chose to put other things first. And you have tolerated division amongst yourselves and grown used to it. And you have not repented of it or fasted for it or sought Me to bring it to an end, but you have tolerated it and you have increased it.

And you have not been My servants first of all in every case. But you have served other people ahead of Me. And you have served this world ahead of Me. And you have served your organizations ahead of Me. But I am God and you are my servant. Why are you not serving Me first of all?

And I know your hearts and I know that many of you love Me and I have compassion on you and I have placed you in a very hard place. But I have placed you there and I call you to account for it. Now humble yourselves before Me. And come to Me, repentant, in fasting, mourning and weeping for the condition of My people, because if you do not humble yourselves now, and seek Me earnestly, then My people will be unprepared for the difficulties that lie ahead.

And I believe that the Lord has a word for us here. I want you to link hands with the people next to you.

And the Lord says to you: Stand in unity with one another and let nothing tear you apart and by no means separate from one another through your jealousies and bitterness and your personal preferences. But hold fast to one another, because I am about to let you undergo a time of severe trial and testing, and you will need to be in unity with one another.

But I tell you this also—I am Jesus, the Victor King—and if you will hold fast to one another, and follow after Me, then I will vindicate My holy name on this earth, and in the sight of the peoples of this earth. It will be manifest and it will be clear and it will be in your lifetime, because I am Jesus, the Victor King, and I have promised you victory.

Second Prophecy

Mourn and weep, for the Body of my Son is broken. Mourn and weep, for the Body of my Son is broken. Come before me with broken hearts and contrite spirits, for the Body of my Son is broken. Come before me with sackcloth and ashes. Come before me with tears and mourning, for the Body of my Son is broken.

I would have made you a new man, but the Body of my Son is broken. I would have made you a light on the mountaintop... a city glorious and splendorous that all would have seen, but the Body of my Son is broken. The light is dim. The people are scattered. The Body of my Son is broken.

I gave all I had and the Body and Blood of my Son is spilled on the earth. The Body of my Son is broken. Turn from the sins of your fathers and walk in the way of my Son. Return to the plan of your Father. Return to the purpose of your God. The Body of my Son is broken. Mourn and weep—for the Body of my Son is broken.

177

The confirmation: The next morning, Sunday, while the non-Catholics gathered in the Convention Center, we Catholics had Mass in Arrowhead Stadium. The Stadium was about a third full, and I seem to remember that there were 123 priests and three bishops concelebrating. The music ministry was great—very upbeat. It was a beautiful sunny morning, just slightly warm.

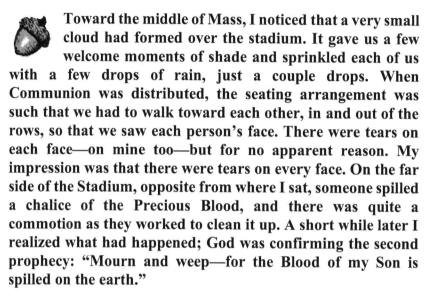 **Toward the middle of Mass, I noticed that a very small cloud had formed over the stadium. It gave us a few welcome moments of shade and sprinkled each of us with a few drops of rain, just a couple drops. When Communion was distributed, the seating arrangement was such that we had to walk toward each other, in and out of the rows, so that we saw each person's face. There were tears on each face—on mine too—but for no apparent reason. My impression was that there were tears on every face. On the far side of the Stadium, opposite from where I sat, someone spilled a chalice of the Precious Blood, and there was quite a commotion as they worked to clean it up. A short while later I realized what had happened; God was confirming the second prophecy: "Mourn and weep—for the Blood of my Son is spilled on the earth."**

Summary: The Elements of Spiritual Growth

As you develop from spiritual childhood to maturity, your family of God activities also evolve. Consider the analogy of football or ballet or modern dance. From beginner to high school to collegiate to professional levels, there is a marked progression, not only in the skills and understanding of the individual players, but also of the training, the coaching, the planning, the individual commitment, the cost, and the rewards and benefits. The same thing is true for the spiritual life and spiritual struggles; it is a lifelong process of healing, growing, and development.

A few key points to help you on the path forward:

1. God's approach to salvation is a team approach; he is working to save all of us, and through our interactions we each play significant parts, for good or ill, in that effort. Each player is unique and important, each has responsibilities, but it is the team that wins the victory. Pick your companions carefully and stay with the team.

2. If you are unhappy with your current spiritual status, remember that some people are spiritual messes. I figure they are probably the folks that drew the tougher demonic opponents. Their struggles keep those demons off the backs of us weaker folk. That is why I suspect God loves them more than the rest of us; he leaves the ninety-nine to go out and rescue these lost sheep.
   Keep in mind:
   a. You are made in God's image with a unique place in his plans. Therefore, you are of great value to him and to the rest of us. Don't get tricked into comparing yourself to others; God made you *you*.
   b. God has a way to heal *all* human ills, so keep looking until you find it.

179

c. God also offers forgiveness for *all* our sins. If you are stuck in habitual sin, keep your focus on the positive things you can do for God and give God time to heal the bad habits.

d. On occasion spiritual growth comes in great, unexpected leaps, but much more frequently it is slow and incremental. Keeping a journal, noting your struggles and prayer requests, is a good way to see the progress that comes from year to year.

3. Looking for spiritual growth the situation always seems to be like the case of the ten virgins waiting for the bridegroom to arrive; the wait always seems much longer that you expect. But he does come and somehow is never late. Stay with the program no matter what—and bring plenty of oil.

4. God never pushes himself upon us. In all we have talked about, it is of primary importance that we ask for his presence and his gifts and invite him into each situation. We must recognize our dependence on God, and we do that by asking and asking again and again.

5. Unity is always important. The team struggles when some players are not performing up to standard, but generally it can better withstand losing a few games than losing players. We are on God's team, and we are playing a long season.

6. Human powers are important in this battle, but the spiritual powers are decisive. "For our struggle is not with flesh and blood but with the principalities, with the powers, with the world rulers of this present darkness, with the evil spirits in the heavens" (Ephesians 6:12). Frequent the sacraments and seek the spiritual gifts; use them, because that is why they are there.

7. "Wait for the Lord, take courage; be stouthearted, wait for the LORD! (Psalm 27:14). "No, the hand of the LORD is not too short to save, nor his ear too dull to hear" (Isaiah 59:1).

180

Your Daily Life

How can you apply these considerations to your daily life? Primarily it is a matter of being faithful to God during the ordinary, day-to-day business of living. As you keep yourself in the good soil, God brings the fruit "in due season." The Church is important. Always keep in mind that you are a brother or sister of Jesus, a member of his personal family, his disciple and therefore much more important than you realize.

More than fifty years ago, I was working for the University of Nevada and my job was to interview people using the state's recreational facilities. At a desolate site in the middle of the desert, I came across a family with six very young children; packed in a station wagon with everything they owned, they were moving to California. They didn't strike me as being very sharp; they certainly were not aware of some of the worldly issues of the Reno area. However, what struck me most and left a lasting impression was the love they showed one another. Those kids were not just clean, happy, and well behaved—they were wrapped in love. It was evident by every word they spoke. You could just feel it. I'm sure this family had no idea they were giving me a standard to follow in the years of my own fatherhood.

A Disciple's Prayer

"I pray not only for them, but also for those who will believe in me through their word, so that they may all be one, as you, Father, are in me and I in you, that they also may be in us, that the world may believe that you sent me. And I have given them the glory you gave me, so that they may be one, as we are one, I in them and you in me, that they may be brought to perfection as one, that the world may know that you sent me, and that you loved them even as you loved me. (John 17:20–23)

Conclusion

Putting it all together, the picture and some next steps

The Church and the Future

 Throughout the course of these pages, we have examined a good number of the elements of Christianity from a perspective born of the Catholic Charismatic Renewal. So, putting them all together, what is that sharp, clear picture of the renewed Church that immerges? Interesting question, right? Let's take a look:

- One key element that immerges from the Charismatic perspective —an element that is all too easy to miss—is balance, in the sense of giving full consideration to all aspects of the Gospel message: spiritual tools, authority, wisdom, and responsibilities. When faced with the struggles of life, both the source of the problem and the solution all too frequently lie in some forgotten truth we just didn't take time to appreciate, something we did fine without for a while. Comparing "What did Jesus emphasize?" with "What is paramount in my life?" can be a very useful exercise for individuals, groups, or even the Church.

- Catholicism, and Christianity in general, is about your direct, unique, very personal relationship with Jesus, a relationship implemented by the actions of the Holy Spirit. That is the essence of the New Covenant, and it bears a number of implications:
  o Each person is uniquely created by God.
  o Each person is uniquely loved by God.
  o Each person has a special, unique place reserved for him or her in God's family. Family membership implies belonging, a personal dignity, being loved, not only by God but also by us, the other family members, and responsibilities. **Too often we tend to underestimate that last word, *responsibilities*. If we must love our**

185

neighbor as ourselves, then we should be as concerned about his or her salvation as our own.

- o Each life is important, and because each person has access to the New and Old Testament gifts of the Holy Spirit, what they can accomplish is virtually unlimited. For example, I once saw the Lord speak through a mentally handicapped young man in a way the moved a whole group of people.

- Next in priority comes our relationship in and with the Church. There can be a bit of confusion here because saying something is of secondary priority tends to imply that its importance is diminished. However, being of second priority does not mean nonessential—in fact, the list of priorities is both long and broad, and all of these priorities are essential. To say it differently, being in secondary priority but connected directly to our first priority, Jesus, makes its importance in daily life grow significantly compared to mistakenly considering it number one. Keep in mind:
  - o The works of the Church—guiding, teaching, healing, the sacraments, etc.—are the community expression, the community parallel, of the gifts of the Holy Spirit described in the individual sense in 1 Corinthians 12, Ephesians 4 and Romans 12. The minister (or individual) invokes the sacrament (or gift) as guidance or need indicates, and the Holy Spirit responds and brings forth the result called for.
  - o The Church is much more than a place where we are spiritually fed and nourished. The Church is also an important field where we are meant to exercise our roles as disciples of the Lord Jesus.

Pope Benedict emphasized[14] this point by stating that the members of the laity hold as much responsibility for the Church as the hierarchy. (Of course, the nature of those responsibilities is different and unique to each person.)

- The key factor that has led to the two previous bullets is the Catholic Charismatic Renewal, but this does not stand alone. The contemporary outpouring of the Holy Spirit's gifts began in Topeka, Kansas in 1901 and with the Azusa Street Revival in Los Angeles, California in 1906, with a wide variety of Christian groups involved. Also important; formal efforts toward Christian unity following Vatican II (that have made substantial progress in both a doctrinal and practical sense), and the increased role of the laity within Catholicism with the concurrent breakdown in unhealthy barriers between hierarchy and laity have all worked together bring into focus the clear realization that God is alive, active, and engaged in combating the strong anti-Christian ideas and politics so current in today's society.
  - o The role of the spiritual gifts has been paramount because the anti-Christian factors have generated a serious degeneration of society's acceptance of authority, whether regarding church, government, or scriptural authority. Thus, the practical, day-to-day witness of the power of the spiritual gifts has been of primary importance in personal conversions and building faith. Direct evidence of God working is especially critical in this skeptical age, and this continues to be a growing trend.

---

[14] Address of His Holiness Benedict XVI to the Opening of the Pastoral Convention of the Diocese of Rome on the Theme: "Church Membership and Pastoral Co-Responsibility," Tuesday, May 26, 2009.

- o It is important to note the official Church position, as expressed in *Iuvenecit Ecclesia*,[15] which expresses that the charismatic gifts of the Church are co-essential with the hierarchical gifts. Likewise, the organizational changes brought about in 2019 in Rome with the advent of the CHARIS panel to promote the Renewal and improve communication between it and Church hierarchy (but not to guide or control it) is noteworthy. Both of these events illustrate the harmony between the "current of grace" which is the Renewal and the official Church.

- Finally, let us close with a note about healing. So far, we have only given a number of witness accounts and a few comments, but hopefully enough to express the great variety of God's healing works and allay some of the misconceptions prevalent in society. However, healing (saving) in the general sense is God's family business; both here in this life and in preparation for the next. It is the business of God the Father, God the Son, and God the Holy Spirit, and thus it is the business of his household, the Church, and his disciples—you and me. Healing is the direct expression of God's love. It is powered by that love and by faith in that love. In the 1970s and 1980s, the witness in the Renewal seemed to focus on simple physical healings, but as time has gone on I have sensed an increasing movement of the Spirit to heal deeper and more serious psychological wounds: persistent doubts, fears, anger, frustration, and the like. God is moving and leaving no stone unturned. So do not fear, despair, or

---

[15] Congregation for the Doctrine of the Faith, Letter *Iuvenescit Ecclesia* to the Bishops of the Catholic Church Regarding the Relationship Between Hierarchical and Charismatic Gifts in the Life and the Mission of the Church; ordered published by Pope Francis, March 14, 2016.

become discouraged by your current situation—God's arm is long enough and strong enough to reach us all.

About the Author

Dr. B. Jeffrey Anderson has served as teacher, organizer and speaker for Lenten missions, parish adult and youth education, RCIA, and a variety of special programs in North Alabama for over forty-five years. He and his wife, Beth, also a speaker and teacher, have been active in the Catholic Charismatic Renewal since 1972. Currently he serves as Director of Education for the diocesan Renewal Organization. The Andersons reside near Huntsville, Alabama. They have nine grown children and eight grandchildren (and still counting).

Until his retirement, Dr. Anderson worked for the National Aeronautics and Space Administration where he was one of the Agency's lead specialists on the effects of natural environment on aerospace system development and flight. His work contributed to numerous programs, including the Space Shuttle, International Space Station, Chandra Telescope and the Constellation Program which began work to return man to the moon and then on to Mars. Dr. Anderson holds a Ph.D. in Physics from the University of Nevada, Reno.

Also by B. Jeffrey Anderson:
The Narrow Road, A Catholic's Path to Spiritual Growth
ISBN 9 781500 480547,   2014
Intercessory Way of the Cross
ISBN 9 781544 007397,   2017

Made in the USA
Columbia, SC
09 March 2023

13472024R00111